THE ART OF PERENNIAL GARDENING

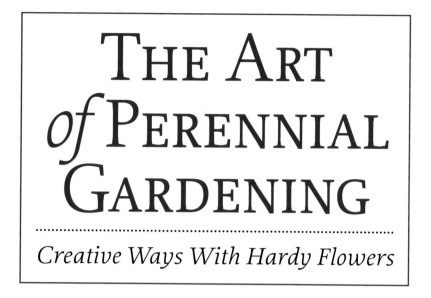

THE ART
of PERENNIAL
GARDENING

Creative Ways With Hardy Flowers

PATRICK LIMA ~ PHOTOGRAPHS BY JOHN SCANLAN

FIREFLY BOOKS

BOOKMAKERS PRESS

A FIREFLY BOOK

Cataloguing-in-Publication Data

Lima, Patrick
       The art of perennial gardening

ISBN 1-55209-219-4

1. Perennials.   I. Title.

SB434.L55   1998   635.9'32   C98-930016-1

Published by
Firefly Books Ltd.
3680 Victoria Park Avenue
Willowdale, Ontario
Canada M2H 3K1

Published in the U.S. by
Firefly Books (U.S.) Inc.
P.O. Box 1338, Ellicott Station
Buffalo, New York 14205

Produced by
Bookmakers Press Inc.
12 Pine Street
Kingston, Ontario K7K 1W1

Design by
Ulrike Bender, Studio Eye

Color separations by
Friesens
Altona, Manitoba

Printed and bound in Canada by
Friesens
Altona, Manitoba

Printed on acid-free paper

Illustration on page 12 by Marta Scythes

*Dedicated with gratitude to the
children of Child Haven,
India and Nepal,
to Bonnie and Fred Cappuccino,
founders of Child Haven International
and to all those involved in an
organization that turns caring and
compassion into action in direct
and simple ways.*

CONTENTS

THE GARDENER'S ART

IN PURSUIT OF BEAUTY

"Everything beautiful impresses us as sufficient to itself."

Henry David Thoreau

FACING PAGE: *One of a garden's charms is that it brings nature close to home.*

ABOVE: *In the democratic world of the garden, the exotic tree peony shares a patch of ground with ordinary chives.*

THE HUMAN SPIRIT RESPONDS NATURALLY to beauty. Confronted with something beautiful, most people feel a spontaneous surge of pleasure, perhaps even gratitude or awe. The aesthetic merit of paintings, furniture, buildings and all the other "stuff of human fashioning" may provoke debate, but an appreciation for the loveliness of Nature seems universal. Rare is the person who does not respond in some way to a starry sky, a mountainscape or a lovely lake, a brilliant sunset, a forest of towering trees, a flower-filled meadow or garden.

My first book about perennials began: "A flower garden is created for pleasure, pure and simple." Gardeners are not alone in finding a frankly sensual enjoyment in the colors, shapes and scents of flowers. And no flowers, someone once said, are as beautiful as those in your own garden. It has to do with relationship and work: the bond

that grows between you and the plants and the place as you design and dig, plant and prune, observe the results of your efforts and make refinements. You exercise your creative muscles and trust that things will turn out more or less as envisioned. A singular satisfaction—often short-lived in the changing world of nature—comes when some imagined scene grows into reality. The artist in you feels fulfilled.

Which is not to say that discouragement never darkens the garden gate. Something or other is invariably being eaten up, dried up, frosted, attacked by mold and mildew; flopping over, falling down, dying back, creeping around, pricking us, sticking us or taxing our backs. But we keep at it—for the flowers, and for beauty.

In June of 1981, my partner John Scanlan and I went on a three-week bicycle tour of English gardens. For

six years, we had been making a garden in an out-of-the-way corner of Ontario's Bruce Peninsula, and our exposure to other gardens had been limited to the pages of gardening books, most of them American volumes from the early 1900s. Now, around every bend was another wondrous garden—a simple rockery full of interesting alpines in front of a row house; an idyllic thatched cottage up to its windowpanes in flowers; perennial borders glimpsed through a wrought-iron gate; roses and clematis dripping from an old stone wall. Almost without knowing it, we absorbed landscaping lessons. On our return home, we began work on a Quiet Garden, an outdoor room enclosed in trelliswork and planted with a silver, green and white theme. We began to introduce more grasses and foliage plants. We also brought back a name for our garden—"Lark-

FACING PAGE: *To appreciate the artistry displayed in a spring gentian, you need to get close to the earth.*

LEFT: *There is a creative imagination at play in the world, an impulse toward beauty and diversity that shows—speaks, some might say— in every aspect of nature.*

whistle"—borrowed from a hand-painted sign pointing down a country lane to we know not where. The name seemed appropriate: Every summer, meadowlarks sing in the scrubby field behind our garden. And "Lark-whistle" surely had a more dulcet ring than the sonorous "Greystone Gardens" we had been considering.

We learned something else in England: Attitude can color a garden as surely as flowers. At one perfectly groomed new garden that centered on a swimming pool, the owner grumbled at every step about the performance of her plants, continually pointing out minor flaws which we would never have noticed. In another garden—old arbors askew, weeds poking through cracks in the paving—the maker, now advanced in years, steered us toward plants that were thriving despite unavoidable neglect, speaking so affectionately about the garden's glory days that what might have been a sad place took on an aura of genuine beauty, a lived-in garden full of char-

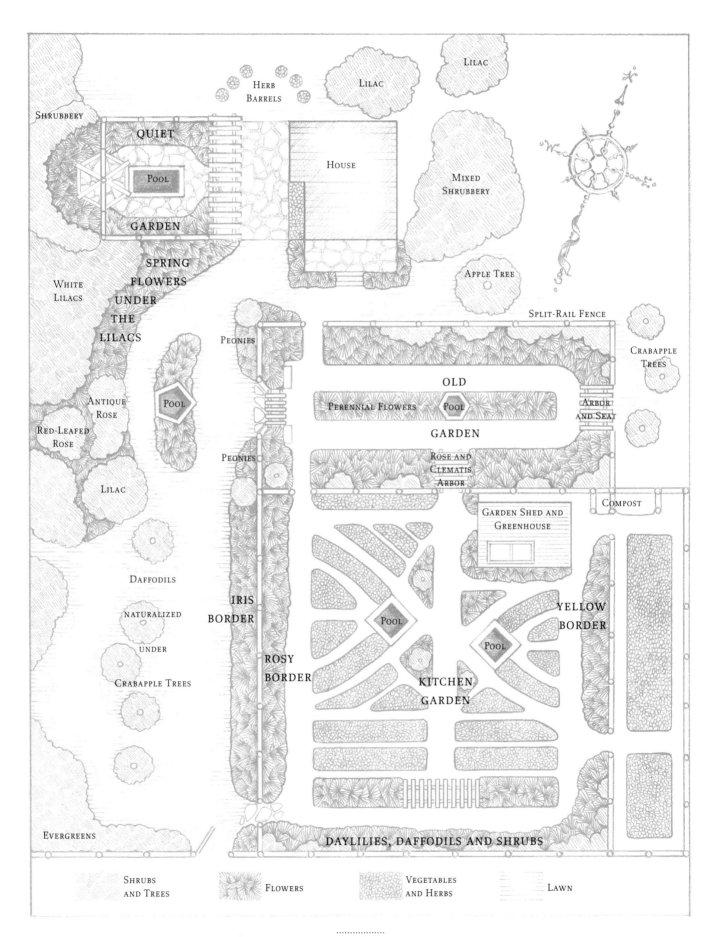

SHRUBBERY

QUIET

Pool

GARDEN

HERB
BARRELS

LILAC

LILAC

LILAC

HOUSE

MIXED
SHRUBBERY

SPRING

FLOWERS

UNDER

THE

LILACS

WHITE
LILACS

APPLE TREE

SPLIT-RAIL FENCE

PEONIES

CRABAPPLE
TREES

ANTIQUE
ROSE

POOL

OLD

Perennial Flowers   POOL

GARDEN

ARBOR
AND SEAT

RED-LEAFED
ROSE

LILAC

PEONIES

ROSE AND
CLEMATIS
ARBOR

COMPOST

GARDEN SHED AND
GREENHOUSE

DAFFODILS

IRIS

BORDER

NATURALIZED

UNDER

POOL

YELLOW
BORDER

CRABAPPLE TREES

ROSY

BORDER

POOL

KITCHEN

GARDEN

EVERGREENS

DAYLILIES, DAFFODILS AND SHRUBS

SHRUBS
AND TREES

FLOWERS

VEGETABLES
AND HERBS

LAWN

acter, history and personal touch.

Every day during the growing season, John and I walk around our garden to see how things are doing. It is just as easy for us to slip into critical mode, focusing on a pining plant, worms on rosebuds, a patch of mildew, some wilted stems—the work, in other words—and to miss all the rest. Invariably, one of us will start by saying, "Those delphiniums are overdue for staking." To which the standard reply is, "It's not *that kind* of tour." A shift in attitude from fretting and criticism to appreciation turns the garden into a different place. You begin to look closely at the fine etching in the throats of blue gentians and to admire the Siberian irises outdoing themselves this year; you poke your nose into a regal lily or a rose, pinch the herbs and inhale their sweet and pungent scents. Nothing keeps you as enthused about gardening as taking time to experience whatever is good and lovely at the moment—and there is always something. Don't worry, the worms and wilt won't go away.

The challenge of gardening—and one of its great attractions—is that we are working with the big forces: changing seasons and shifting winds, the earth, sun and rain in all their moods. A gardener can do only so much; after that, things are quite literally in other hands. In our forgetful day-to-day way, we tend to think of the garden as entirely our own handiwork. By toiling away, getting the place the way you like it, you feel in charge. Until the summer morning when you wander into the dawn-lit garden and find dew-hung spider's webs slung between stalks and glistening water drops like beads, caught on the leaves of Lady's mantle. You marvel at silken poppies freed from the tight green wraps that held them yesterday and now loose on the breeze. Time stands still as a hummingbird hovers above crowns of bergamot. Tall grasses sway and rip-

ple as if caressed by an invisible hand. For a moment, you forget about the staking that should have been done yesterday. You stop and take in the garden's beauty, both the work of your hands and not. You feel restored, refreshed, reminded of "the blessings of the Earth" and "all things bright and beautiful," as the old hymns say.

Change will come, problems will arise. Eventually, you become reconciled to the fact that clematis sometimes wilts and drought happens. In a garden, romantic notions never stop bumping into earthy realities; back and limbs may not be equal to flights of imagination.

But once caught by a vision, gardeners have a tendency to persist. We don't mind getting dirty—grubbing about in flowerbeds is what we do for recreation. We can be perversely happy rooting out our old nemesis bindweed or weaving thorny rose branches through supports at

peril to hands and arms—"There *are* gloves in the shed, you know." We're on a kind of mission. John tells me that when he first saw the flat hayfield that was to become our garden, he thought, "I'd like to make something beautiful here." Which comes as close to a gardener's creed as anything does.

LEFT: *New plants will always pique a gardener's curiosity, but horticultural traditions are kept alive in such flowers as hollyhocks.*

The Art of Perennial Gardening

EVOLUTION

....

I wonder if our experience at Lark-whistle isn't typical of what might be called the evolution of a gardener. In every gardener, there lives both a collector and an artist. The collector can't resist squeezing in one more perennial or shrub; the artist wants to focus on relationships, color combinations, the overall effect. The collector bubbles with the enthusiasm of a scientist or child for something new observed close-up, while the artist longs for those satisfying stand-back moments when colors, forms and textures interplay in a beautiful way. Curiosity, vision: even though they sometimes tug in different directions, you need both. By way of compromise, the collector is often given *carte blanche* for a few seasons, after which the artist steps in to sort out the confusion—always allowing the collec-

tor new plants, of course, in exchange for promises to dig.

In the early years, most gardeners are absorbed in getting to know new plants—reading about them, searching them out, tending them. The goal is to see in living color, in our own gardens, flowers lauded in books and praised by friends. Diligently, we research requirements. Where we put a plant depends on what it needs to thrive. How it might look in relation to its neighbors comes as an afterthought—if at all. So what if purple phlox and salmon tiger lilies are blooming side by side? The important thing is that they are alive and well. We must be doing something right.

At this stage, the focus is on individual plants and how best to grow them. Bringing each to bloom is thrill enough: We're in the "collecting" phase. The first time Carpathian

harebells popped open in our garden, I thought I had never seen a lovelier blue. When the first small purple stars of *Daphne mezereum* twinkled out one April day, I caught their scent with amazement—so powerful from such a little bloom in such cool air. It happened over and over again, each new flower a surprise.

Gradually, we begin to gain confidence. We discover that most perennials are going to do well if put in a suitable spot and given a modicum of care; some will even overachieve mightily. We become less concerned about practical things like soil and more preoccupied with overall effects. Pictorial possibilities tickle our imaginations. Wouldn't it be gorgeous to have a dark violet clematis running through that bush of pink roses? How about tucking a few blue forget-me-nots over top of the yellow tulip bulbs we just buried? This kind

FACING PAGE: *Once we get to know our plants and how best to grow them, our imaginations are free to explore artistic possibilities, including a host of intriguing color combinations.*

LEFT: *A garden picture is any combination of plants that have been chosen for form, texture and color to bring out the best in one another.*

of thinking marks a shift from growing plants to making a garden. The "artistic" phase has begun.

In her second book, *Colour in My Garden* (1918), American garden writer Louise Beebe Wilder describes the symptoms: "We become obsessed by what John Sedding calls the 'malady of the ideal,' we are haunted by visions of exquisite colors in perfect harmony, and our aim is henceforth to make the garden a place for broad survey as well as for minute scrutiny; to enjoy not only the indi-vidual flower but to make the most of it in relation to other flowers." Now we seldom decide to introduce a plant into the garden without first picturing how it will look as part of a larger composition.

Not that we ignore soil and siting—squeezing plants into inhospitable places defeats the purpose. Creative gardening builds on a foundation of practical know-how, the earthy prerequisites for healthy growth. And then the imagination is free to play.

QUESTIONS OF AESTHETICS

Gertrude Jekyll, England's turn-of-the-century master gardener, once wrote that it had taken her 20 years to decide what was most worth striving for in the garden. "To devise living pictures," she concluded, "with simple well-known flowers is the best thing to do in gardening." It's a motto I wholeheartedly endorse—partly out of necessity. The climate of our zone 4 central-Ontario locale automatically eliminates a lot of possibilities, especially some of the glorious shrubs and small trees—azaleas, ornamental cherries, flowering dogwoods, even forsythias—that play such an integral role in warmer landscapes. What we are left with—and believe me, I'm not complaining—is a host of "simple well-known flowers." And the best of them are perennials, plants that retreat underground

over winter, protected from the worst cold by an insulating cover of frozen earth and snow. Along with spring bulbs, hardy roses and tough shrubs such as lilacs, mock orange, spireas, viburnums and such, perennials supply all the colors, forms and textures we need to compose garden pictures—enough to keep us mucking around for years.

Someone summed up creative gardening as "the decorative employment of flowers—their arrangement and relation in the garden so as to bring about beautiful pictures." A garden picture is any combination of plants chosen to bring out the best in one another: a wave of silver artemisia in front of salmon Oriental poppies; round, billowing hardy geraniums, pink and white, chosen to accentuate the stiff verticality of blue Siberian irises; lavender and cherry tulips (rather than scarlet and yel-

low) in the same frame of vision as a pink flowering crabapple.

Like anything else, picture-making can get out of hand and be overdone to the point of artificiality. A gardener works with living stuff, not static furniture and fabric. Plan your pictures, but welcome surprises—wayward seedlings may teach you something about color and lend idiosyncratic notes to a too careful scheme. They might even make you rich. I love the story of the English gardener (this was in the 1910s, when color scheming was at a zenith of popularity) who ordered crimson Oriental poppies from nurseryman Amos Perry to provide the proper touch of brilliance in a flower border carefully orchestrated in shades of pink and red, with flesh tones at either end and working up to a crescendo of deep red in the middle. One June day, Mr. Perry received an

irate call from the gardener, who was furious that "a nasty fat white poppy" had appeared in the place reserved for red. Now it so happened that Amos Perry had been breeding Oriental poppies for years. To date, he had succeeded in producing a fine pink 'Mrs. Perry'—but his heart was set on a white one. Hardly daring to hope, Perry went to visit his angry customer, and sure enough, there stood a white Oriental poppy in full bloom. All apologies, the nurseryman offered some nice red montbretia in exchange for the transgressor—a poppy that has come down to gardens today as 'Perry's White,' probably earning Perry and his heirs a tidy sum in the bargain.

Creative gardening begins with questions, some inner looking. Realistically, how much garden can I look after? (Trouble is, you don't know until you've outdug yourself, but never mind.) What kinds of plants am I drawn to in other gardens and in picture books? Does my nature demand formality and control, or do I yearn for wild-looking randomness or something in between, along the lines of Vita Sackville-West's "controlled untidiness"? In the cause of picture-making, can I resist the urge

to collect in favor of an artistic vision? Which is to say, can I forgo one each of "the latest" for fewer plants chosen for their ensemble effect? Or is the collector's impulse so strong that I'm much happier with variety and to heck with how they look together? And the "funnest" question of all: What are my favorite colors?

Other questions are more practical. For better or worse, you start with the given, so the first thing to ask may be: What is out there now? The artistic gardener also needs to find out which flowers bloom at the same time in the area; if you need an excuse to go on garden tours, you can always call it research. Which plants enjoy similar conditions of soil and exposure? Which are reliably hardy? How will the colors of potential companions accord or clash? Will there be fresh foliage after the flowers are gone?

No one sits down, answers a series of questions and, voilà, finds the garden is sorted out once and for all. The landscape changes. You change. Gardening is about process. At heart, it is a romantic quest, a striving after an ideal. The goal is simply beauty, a kind of possible/impossible dream that begins to slip away even as you achieve it.

The Art of Perennial Gardening

CREATIVE GARDENING

PRINCIPLES OF DESIGN

"There is no spot of ground,
however arid, bare or ugly,
that cannot be tamed into such a
state as may give the impression
of beauty and delight."

GERTRUDE JEKYLL

FACING PAGE: *Using contrasting plant forms while blending colors is a time-honored approach to flower gardening.*

ABOVE: *A mix of perennials, woody plants and annuals—here, monkshood, roses and pansies—is typical of gardens today.*

My guess is that few gardeners begin a day outdoors with earnest thoughts about principles of design—the need to repeat plants, contrast forms and harmonize colors. If you are anything like us, you go outside, look around and get started on whatever draws your attention—unpruned roses starting to sprout, a chaotically overgrown bed or the urgent transplanting of some expensive treasure that caught your eye at the nursery weeks ago and has grown rootbound waiting for you to perform that most common of garden miracles—creating space where none existed before. Much of gardening is impulsive, acts of uprooting and rearranging that we like to think of as intuitive rather than desperate. But spur-of-the-moment decisions do not come out of the blue. They are influenced by something you've read or last year's notes, by experiments and observa-tions; and by that compelling fusion of imagination and longing that seems to drive gardeners.

Design principles tend to emerge from what you do, rather than the other way round. By plan or whim, you make a move. A few months later, you stand back and look; if you like what you see, a principle begins to form—something to think about next time. After a few years, more of your decisions are based on past successes and a kind of loop begins: good results leading to principles leading to the kind of garden you enjoy. Reflecting on what has turned out well at Larkwhistle, it is clear that certain principles of design have been guiding our choices—at least, I like to think so now that I have to tell you what they are. My intention in setting down a list of principles is not to prescribe a precise method but rather to suggest things you might consider as you begin a new planting or renovate a bed.

Although this book is about perennials, it should be remembered that a mixture of elements—shrubs, ornamental trees, vines *and* flowers—is usually preferable to strict segregation. Although perennials predominate at Larkwhistle, none of our flowerbeds is entirely herbaceous. Each holds a shrub or two, a small tree, a rosebush or a climbing vine. Besides drawing the eye upward, these woody plants give a garden a more settled and permanent appearance. They also bestow a visible history. Perennials look more or less the same from year to year; when they deteriorate, we dig them up for division and renewal. But shrubs and trees show their age in interesting ways—a twist of trunk, increasing heights, an expanding canopy of leaves, lichen-encrusted limbs. Set in key places, the crabapple and cherry trees, lilacs, mock oranges and rugosa roses, the evergreens and vines demarcate the shape and layout of our garden and give definition to a space that would otherwise be flat and bare after perennials have been cut down in fall. Flowers are the finishing touches, ephemeral by nature and less serious; with flowers, we get to play, juggle colors and change the face of the garden in ways we could never contemplate with heavyweight shrubs and trees.

At one time, perennials were grown in long, wide borders backed by a fence, wall or hedge. The results were spectacular—and still are where such borders are maintained—but few arrangements are as tricky to tend. I speak from experience. Inspired by old gardening books, John and I laid out five such borders in our enthusiastic youth, spaces that mysteriously grow longer and wider with every passing season. Unless you wade bodily into the borders—more like hop, skip and jump into them—you cannot do the work. And so you gather your stakes and twine and pick your way toward the delphiniums in the back row—only to find you've forgotten scissors. Turning on a dime, you tiptoe out, fetch the scissors and neglect to bring the trowel you need to turf out that stubbornly rooted dandelion. In and out you go, all the while worrying that you'll accidentally crush some tender shoot with all that pirouetting and sidestepping.

By contrast, all our recent plantings are in smaller island beds of various shapes that we tend from the surrounding paths or with a step or two into the bed. Each bed is a nicely circumscribed canvas suitable for two or three pictures. With some thought given to the colors and forms in adjacent plots, a series of smaller beds can have the same impact as a big border, but without the strain. The composition of those beds will always be idiosyncratic, the result of each gardener's

imagination applied to a particular site. A few principles of design may help guide the creative process.

REPETITION

"Horticulture," wrote Maurice Hewlett, "is, next to music, the most sensitive of the fine arts." The comparison is intriguing. The beauty of music comes in part from a recognizable melody carried through a piece, emerging and reemerging. Such a melody, or theme, sets up a pattern of anticipation and satisfaction in the listener. In a garden, something similar happens through the repetition of theme plants. The eye enjoys traveling out over an area, then returns,

only to start off again. What it comes back to is the familiar element—the repeated plants. A unified effect is more pleasing and restful than a busy spottiness. By using the same (or similar) plants in several places, you achieve a kind of visual circularity that draws a planting together. Repetition helps bring a sense of cohesion to the diversity found in most gardens, a unity that is experienced without being too obvious.

At the front of one of our long perennial beds grow two stretches of gray-leafed lamb's ears (*Stachys byzan-*

FACING PAGE: *Repeated patches of woolly lamb's ears help unify a mixed border in Larkwhistle's Old Garden.*

LEFT: *As acanthus, or bear's breeches, amply illustrates, dramatic form and interesting textures in both foliage and flower may be just as useful in the hands of the creative garden as color is.*

The Art of Perennial Gardening

tina), spaced about 25 feet (7.5 m) apart. Even though the plants behind them are a mixed lot, the eye moves naturally from one patch of lamb's ears to the other and back, taking in the whole border in a fluid way as it travels. The silver foliage catches the eye better than green, strengthening the visual flow.

In our Rosy Border, repeated clumps of Siberian irises, their leafy sheaves standing fresh all season, help hold things together. A background hedge of rugosa roses—and a hedge is nothing more than one plant repeated—also unifies this bed, while along the edge, patches of dianthus are broken at regular intervals by mounds of ornamental catmint. At the front of our Yellow Border, several groups of 'Moonshine' yarrow and 'Blue Beauty' catmint draw the eye along and back in the same way. All this may sound formal, but the effect

is naturalistic. Nature, after all, is forever repeating plants in any expanse of wild land.

Repetition also works on either side of a path. In the Old Garden, two groups of lavender grow across from each other, edging two facing beds. As you go down the path, your vision meanders from one side to the other—lavender here and there. But you have to be careful: repeating plants too precisely can give an impression of stiff regimentation. Subtlety is part of beauty, and sometimes an irregular spacing of repeated plants is preferable to exact intervals.

The character of repeated plants also makes a difference. On either side of a walkway leading to a front door, upright junipers are dramatic and exclamatory, almost sentrylike. Very different in effect are four clumps of ornamental grass planted at the four corners of a small raised pool,

itself directly in the middle of our Old Garden. The leaves of grass arch and sway, a movement that softens the effect; in the same setting, stiffer plants would look far too orderly.

Think of repeated plants as a ribbon weaving through a flowerbed in the same way that a band of color weaves through a tapestry, not continuously but surfacing here and there and tying things together. Not every perennial is suitable for the purpose. Choose plants that have a definite presence on their own and remain as clumps of good foliage all season—you don't want the ribbon going threadbare by July. The principle of repetition can be applied not only in individual beds but in the landscape as a whole, with certain shrubs or trees planted in several places. But, as always, a good thing can be overdone: repeating every element in the garden tends to look arti-

FACING PAGE: *Shrubs, roses, ornamental trees, evergreens and flowers grown together create a more interesting garden than does a strict segregation of elements.*

LEFT: *For some gardeners, color harmony may be more appealing than strong contrasts.*

ficial. Later on, we'll see that the repetition of colors, or shades of a color, also pulls a garden together.

GROUPING

A related principle, grouping is the repetition of one kind of plant in a given space. In a small garden, you might well use one each of this and that and end up with a satisfying ensemble, especially if you choose plants with pleasing outlines and decorative leaves. But even in a small area, a few grouped plants lend stability. As a rule, one each of a lot of different plants causes the eye to bounce around. Where space allows, I find it preferable to plant two or three or more of a particular perennial together, since a mass of one flower or one kind of foliage compels the eye to pause instead of moving on. Grouping also brings out the distinct character of a plant, whether wispy or bold-leafed, soft-colored or shocking, mounding or upright. Most obviously, grouping intensifies color—the difference between a small daub and an important patch of color on a canvas.

To avoid the lurching-eye syndrome, small plants in large beds should always be grouped. Picture 12 different perennials, each a foot (30 cm) apart, along the front of a 12-foot (3.6 m) bed, and you can see why. But limit your choices to three or four varieties, and the eye relaxes and moves easily from one patch to the next. Grouping also strengthens the impact of perennials that appear weedy and insubstantial as solo players. Add several more leopard's bane, purple rockcress or *Salvia* x *superba* to the one you have, and see how a plant that looked ho-hum doing a solo turn takes on greater presence. (Of course,

plenty of perennials know they look better *en masse* and take on the job of expansion as a personal mission. You'd be ill-advised to plant three yarrows, for example, when one will creep into every bit of unoccupied earth within root-reach, forcing you to take drastic measures.)

The number of plants in a group depends on their size and the available space. In larger beds, I usually plant small perennials in groups of five or seven, medium-sized ones in threes or fives and tall plants in groups of three. Odd-numbering, a suggestion borrowed from old books, is thought to banish any hint of formality; twos and fours are thought to look, well, too *even*. The shape of a group may also give an impression of either symmetry or naturalness. I might set three plants in a crooked triangle or a slightly arcing line but not in a row. Five plants are arranged

with three forward and two staggered behind, and so on. If this sounds complicated, remember that most plants billow or tumble or arch out. Arranged in overlapping groups—loose ovals, elongated fish shapes, wonky rectangles or any shape beyond straight lines, sharp squares or circles—perennials will flow together, filling the space naturally (even if you start with two or four). It was English garden artist Gertrude Jekyll who first suggested planting in long skinny "drifts" that leave smaller gaps when the flowering of one group is done and adjacent plants lean in and bridge the space.

The distance between plants in a group is important (I remind myself each time I'm tempted to squeeze one more little guy into a border bursting at the seams). Adequate elbowroom gives rise to robust, healthy growth; crowding leads to weak, spindly

stems. When calculating planting distances, think in terms of dwarf, medium and tall plants: dwarfs grow from 6 to 18 inches high (15 to 45 cm)—up to knee-high; medium height is from 18 inches to 3 feet (45 cm to 1 m), or roughly knee- to waist-high; tall plants reach 3 feet (1 m) and up, or from your waist to way over your head. Space dwarf perennials 1 foot (30 cm) apart, medium-sized plants 18 inches (45 cm) apart and tall ones 2 feet (60 cm) from each other. Which is not to say I take a ruler into the garden—that kind of precision is seldom necessary. The body is the origin of most measurement, and when you are on your hands and knees, what is handier than your hand? A hand span, for all but the octave-and-a-half concert pianists among us, is about 6 to 8 inches (15 to 20 cm). A little either way is not critical, but better to err on the side of generous spacing.

All this talk of grouping does not rule out some plants standing alone in important spots as specimens. In full flower, a single torch lily, or red-hot poker (*Kniphofia* spp), is a spectacular sight; the fact that it may die on you one not-so-fine winter also discourages massing. In our Yellow Border, three plants of *Kniphofia* 'Primrose Beauty' stand as specimens at intervals. Which takes us back to our first principle: perennials chosen as specimens are often ideal repeaters because for both roles, you want substantial plants of fine foliage that stand out from the crowd.

CONTRASTING PLANT FORMS

Before juxtaposing any plants, take a moment to consider their forms, and whenever feasible, position those of differing shapes as neighbors. A strategy that conveys immediate visual interest, contrasting forms is one of the simplest design principles to follow. Often it happens by accident. One way to

FACING PAGE: *The effectiveness of contrasting plant forms is abundantly evident when delphiniums, baby's breath and lilies are grown together.*

LEFT: *Bergenia's leathery ping-pong-paddle leaves are even more pronounced when contrasted with upright lilies, here a cultivar named 'Embarrassment.'*

appreciate a design principle is to picture its opposite: a bed composed, for example, of only plants with simple straight-edged leaves—grasses, yuccas, irises, daylilies, crocosmia, and the like. When the bloom is off, the view is as uninteresting as a hayfield, but add a few perennials with different contours, and the picture changes for the better.

By form, I mean a plant's overall configuration, its shape or outline both in and out of flower. Some plants are round and billowing—

hummocks, mounds, cushions. Cushion spurge and *Artemisia* 'Silver Mound' are well named, and hardy geraniums are mounding plants *par excellence.* Others are arching in form, with leaves ascending then bending gracefully toward the ground. Many ornamental grasses have this arching profile, as do daylilies. Still others grow upright (or, as catalogs like to say, "stiff and erect"). In this aspiring group are snakeroot, spiked veronica, obedient plant and delphiniums. The handsome, lasting leaves of the Siber-

straight leaves of desert candles (*Eremurus*) precede its spires of bloom. But to add interest, you encounter plants like ornamental catmints, with mounding foliage and upright flower stems, or exotic bear's breeches (*Acanthus spinosus*), whose broad thistlelike leaves fan out below spikes of weird blooms. Lupins also fan and spire.

Here are a few examples of forms that work well together:

- Mounding geraniums in front of upright Siberian irises or fanning peonies.
- Arching daylilies next to upright spiked veronica (as a bonus, veronica's stained-glass blues are lovely with the fruit colors of daylilies).
- Tall, upright-to-arching grasses behind fanning astilbe.
- Spires of lupins or the candles of mulleins are classic with the billowing roundness of bearded irises.
- Spiky perennial salvia next to fanning, flat-topped yarrow—a favorite combination in English borders.
- A rounded peony (out of flower) in front of an upright delphinium; the peony also hides the delphinium's shabby lower leaves.
- The broad fans of bergenia leaves in front of arching daylilies.
- Fanning hostas in front of upright snakeroot.

LASTING LEAVES

Flowers are alluring by nature, and new gardeners, like bees, are naturally drawn to them. But as Louise Beebe Wilder whimsically noted, many of the most glamorous perennials—tulips, daffodils, Oriental poppies, bearded irises and delphiniums—"lose all pride in their appearance as soon as flowering is accomplished. They go to seed most untidily, quite lose their figures and make no effort at all to grow old with dignity and grace." Sooner or later, probably one dry day in August, you look around and, after humming a

ian irises fall somewhere between upright and arching.

Then there are perennials that fan, their leaves spreading out laterally. Astilbes are elegant fanners, hostas are broadly fanning, and most yarrows have a horizontal line of foliage and flowers. Others with a fanning form include columbines, the pink cornflower *Centaurea dealbata rosea*, all of the meadow rues (*Thalictrum* spp) and various bleeding hearts (*Dicentra* spp).

Foliage often gives a plant its basic form, but some perennials are informed by flowers. None of the gypsophilas have leaves worth discussing, but the myriad tiny flowers threaded like beads on wiry stems always arrange themselves in a billowing cloud. The mottled leaves of coral bells—one of Sackville-West's "see-through flowers"—fan out at ground level, but the profusion of tiny flowers on thin straight stems count for more (except in newer cultivars bred for showy foliage). Often form is carried through a plant: the

bar of "Where have all the flowers gone…" recognize the value of foliage. Where leaves last, the garden looks lush and lively (which is easier read than said). Late summer is a good time to survey flowerbeds, your own and others, and make a list of perennials that continue to give a good account of themselves in the foliar department. Endurance is part of the picture, but put a star beside plants whose leaves are not only lasting but decorative in their own

right. It is always wise to allot a fair bit of space to such plants, even if it means replacing a few favorites that flower and flee.

My own list of perennials that remain presentable once the bloom is off runs as follows: acanthus, silver-leafed achilleas such as 'Moonshine' and 'Goldplate,' aconite, fan-leafed alchemilla, Japanese anemones, silvery artemisias, elegant astilbe, leather-leafed bergenia, daylilies, globe thistle, many grasses, hardy geraniums (among the best), hostas, Siberian and other nonbearded irises, lamb's ears (once the scruffy spent flower stalks are cut off), meadow rue, peonies, various sedums, snake-root and tall veronicastrum. Many herbs keep their leaves, none as beautifully as rue and the green and white

variegated apple mint; where it proves hardy, bronze fennel makes a sheer veil of wispy foliage. Unless hit with mildew, monarda and phlox also qualify.

Drawing a clear line between path or lawn and flowerbed, long-lasting leaves are especially important at the edge. Luckily, there is no shortage of low-growing perennials for edging purposes: long-lived rockcress and creeping phlox, gray-leafed dianthus (or pinks) and ornamental catmints, evergreen candytuft, flowerless 'Silver Carpet' lamb's ears and dainty coral bells—some of the newer *Heuchera* have gorgeous leaves. Shorter versions of hardy *Geranium sanguineum* are sterling edgers, long-flowering and always green and tidy; look for dwarf 'John Eisley,' the slightly taller (8-inch/20-cm) 'Max Frei'—both deep magenta-rose—and the blush-pink *G. s. striatum*, once known as *G.s. lancastriense*.

FIELD OF VIEW

"For goodness sake," our guide said as she took us around her garden, "don't keep peering down at each blessed plant in turn. Look up once in a while. The garden is meant to be seen overall—a series of pictures." And she was right. Curious novices at the time, we could not help zooming in on individual plants, many of them new to us, and pestering our host with questions: What's its name? Is it hardy? How long does it bloom? Can you spare a piece? But looking up, we could see how the imagination of this gardener had shaped and colored the place as a whole.

Just as crimson is crimson on each painter's palette, a cornflower is the same from one garden to the next. Charm and originality arise from the way each gardener combines plants according to his or her unique vision. The eye, like an adjustable camera lens, is capable of seeing close-up, mid-range or long-view. As we realize

FACING PAGE: *The differing leaf shapes and colors of spiny sea holly and arching crocosmia set each other off uncommonly well.*

LEFT: *Big blue hosta leaves are a prominent feature in our Quiet Garden all season long.*

that a garden is only as beautiful as the ensemble effect—the sum of its parts—we begin to widen our sights.

I have yet to sit down with colored pencils and graph paper and draw up a comprehensive plan for a flower border. It's a task I find both daunting and nitpicking, too grand and too detailed at the same time. My hunch is that most gardeners compose in a more piecemeal fashion, finding a compromise between an inflexible master plan and making a garden one plant at a time with whatever strikes one's fancy at the moment. After leafing through my written notes or rummaging through mental files for the perfect plan hatched last summer (and not committed to paper), I usually heft my small spade and compose on the spot, thoughts focused on the few square yards within sight and reach. Which is also how I look at the garden: taking in the area within view—more than individual plants, less than the whole place—the way you might take a photograph. Of course, you never stop peering closely at new plants or gazing off into misty vistas.

A mid-range view usually encompasses about a 7-foot (2 m) length, space enough for a perennial picture of some complexity. Composing within such a frame encourages you to pay attention to plants that will be immediate neighbors—those you will see together—and worry less about what is going on down the way. In a longer border, a few repeater plants and an overall color scheme will unify the collection.

I find this "framed" approach especially useful when rearranging plants in an established border. The prospect of taking apart a big bed is enough to scare me off, but tackling one section at a time is both possible and satisfying. Starting with a general idea about color, I focus on an area, removing, adding, shifting. I think about which plants will show up well as companions; one move suggests the next. A

series of pictures, each composed within a limited field of view, adds up to a bed—and a garden.

SUCCESSION OF BLOOM

Flowers from April to October—some gardeners turn to perennials with high hopes of constant color. But let's be clear about what succession of bloom means. Short of what has been called "expert pot-dropping," there is no earthly way to have an ordinary perennial bed that is alight from end to end nonstop from early spring until late fall. On the other hand, it's a reasonable goal to expect some flowers to be coming on as others fade, with plenty of green to tide things over. The way to achieve succession is to think in terms of *phases of bloom*, not precisely spring, summer and fall, but five or six overlapping waves. You then choose several different perennials for each phase. It may be tempting to put all the flowers of one phase together in one area for dramatic effect. But a better plan is

FACING PAGE: *Precisely because they are so different in all respects, 'Mahogany' peony and Lychnis flos-jovis are a striking match; their colors might be described as a harmonious contrast.*

LEFT: *This bed of bergamot, phlox and agapanthus is enhanced by the presence of a small peegee hydrangea tree and the splashy foliage of zebra grass.*

to distribute perennials that bloom at the same time throughout a bed—a patch of late-May color here, there and over there. Drawn immediately to whatever is in bloom, the eye registers an impression of color throughout.

In our Old Garden, the area where we first planted perennials, different flowers unfold from April to October. Describing the whole area in detail would stretch to pages. But one section may illustrate the potential for six phases of flowers in a relatively small space. To the right of the

entrance arbor is an L-shaped corner bed fronted by a comfortable bench. A rambling 'Dorothy Perkins' rose weaves up a trellis attached to the arbor. In the opposite corner, you see a bush of 'Stanwell's Perpetual' rose— actually three bushes planted close together to look like one. At the back, casting a light shade in the hot afternoon, stands a wide-armed crabapple tree, the double pink 'Bechtal's Crab.'

The rock-raised edge of this bed is covered by a shawl of double-flowered arabis, a long-lived showy plant that

The Art of Perennial Gardening

cal contrast to billowing white baby's breath, a few ivory Turk's-cap lilies and a patch of red bergamot in the foreground. July now, and clusters of small pink 'Dorothy Perkins' roses are hanging from the trellis. With any luck, a violet clematis is wending its way through the roses.

One more phase awaits. Spring's daffodils are sandwiched between three clumps of peach and apricot daylilies and five plants of white phlox behind them. Now in August, the daylilies and phlox are companioned by spires of monkshood, both blue-and-white and deep violet, in

stays green year-round. Sprouting thickly through the arabis in April are masses of purple and lavender-striped crocuses. The crocuses are succeeded by clumps of white daffodils midway back. And just behind the arabis, seeming to float on its frothy white in May, are crimson goblets of the crimson early tulips 'Couleur Cardinal.' Most years, the daffodils, tulips and arabis bloom together, a trio embellished lately by fountains of turquoise Virginia bluebells, the seed blown in or dropped by birds. As bulbs fade, the

crabapple flowers, followed in early June by old clumps of white Oriental poppies and the fragrant lace caps of valerian reaching into the lower boughs of the crab; valerian takes care of itself (and then some) in the back row. Four phases so far, and summer has just begun.

Mid-June, and the bed is full of green and promise. After the poppies depart, there is a lull before 'Stanwell's Perpetual' breaks into scented blush-pink roses. Soon a blue delphinium is shooting skyward, a verti-

FACING PAGE, TOP RIGHT: *The beginning: Spring brings a mass of crocuses to this L-shaped bed.*

FACING PAGE, LEFT: *The second phase comes in May with the flowering of double arabis, early red tulips and white daffodils.*

FACING PAGE, BOTTOM RIGHT: *In late May, the single 'Bechtal's Crab' takes pride of place; it is soon followed by clumps of white poppies and the blooming of several roses.*

LEFT: *The last phase: Daylilies, phlox and red bergamot bring this hard-working bed to a close in late summer.*

the background. September sees a few phlox flowers and the occasional daylily flickering out. Soon we'll be cutting back and spreading a dressing of compost over a piece of earth that has given a full season of beauty.

This corner—a collection of "simple well-known flowers" composed as a series of changing pictures—tells us a few things. Two or three different flowers blooming at the same time are sufficient to make a picture. Even one element, massed or strategically placed—the crocuses, the poppies or the crabapple tree—carries a bed along. The constructed pieces—fence, arbor, bench—add character and a sense of containment. A few woody plants—shrubs, roses, flowering trees—lend height and stability as well as winter interest. And finally, a color scheme need not be consistent throughout the whole season: in this bed, purple gives way to red and white; then pink and blue enter the picture, followed by peach, violet and white. The best thing about it? Everything comes back next year.

The Art of Perennial Gardening

Color
in the Garden

EXPLORING THE FLORAL SPECTRUM

*"Beauty deprived of its
proper foil ceases to be
enjoyed as beauty, just as light
deprived of all shadow ceases
to be enjoyed as light."*

John Ruskin

FACING PAGE: *Siberian irises: Blue with
lavender undertones is a cool, pacific
color that blends with all others.*

ABOVE: *Rudbeckia 'Irish Eyes': Sunny
yellow is one of the ubiquitous
flower colors.*

GOOD FOLIAGE AND CONTRASTING FORMS
are all well and good, but ultimately,
a flower garden is about color: beds
and borders spilling over with watery
blue irises, opalescent peonies, crimson daisies, inky delphiniums and
clematis, radiant yellow daffodils,
bold red poppies, flame daylilies,
pink pinks, rose roses, white lilies
washed with the hue of watered
wine, the iridescent azure of meconopsis. After half a year of somber
gray, green, brown and white, color
comes as a celebration.

Flowers have been part of human
life for so long that some of their
names have become names for colors:
rose, violet, lavender, mauve (which
is French for mallow), lilac, fuchsia,
gentian, primrose—the very words
call up lovely images. Some scenes
etch themselves in memory. One
winter about 25 years ago, I was
roaming around Greece, lugging my
backpack from island to island, soaking up sights and sunshine. Greece
does not have winter the way Canada
has winter, but even so, the February
landscape was a subdued study in
gray rocks, faded green slopes, silver
olive trees, brown and white goats—
more than pleasant, considering the
slushy alternative back home. As
March rolled in, the days grew
warmer. Spring was on the way. One
morning, as I hiked along a stony
footpath on the way to an ancient
hilltop chapel, I caught sight of a single red poppy in the distance, glowing like an ember in the middle of a
grassy field. The vivid scarlet circle
held me rapt, almost burning its way
into my vision as the surrounding
field faded into the background. One
flower, but I still remember it, which
says something about the impact of
color. I only wish I could have stayed
to see the whole field ignite.

Like most people, I have favorite
colors, but when it comes to flowers,
my tastes are wide and inclusive.
Every hue is welcome, from the
black-centered shocking magenta

pink of *Geranium psilostemon*—as
improbable a color experiment as
nature ever undertook—to the weird
salmon-orange of tiger lilies and the
heavenly blue of delphiniums. Only a
few colors rankle my sensibilities.
Certain lacquer-red tulips with spi-
dery blue-black centers boldly outlined in yellow scare me off. And the
screaming scarlet-orange of *Papaver
orientale* comes on a bit strong,
although it calms down when companioned with cream irises, lacy
white valerian and plenty of green. I

have to agree with the early writer
who said, "My own feeling in the
matter of flower colors is that none is
bad if given a happy association." It's
a question of company—and you get
to be a harmless tyrant, inviting or
evicting as you please.

One of the themes of this book is
the "happy association" of flower colors. For me, some degree of harmony
is always happier than stark and bla-
tant contrasts. But the sense of which
colors sing together is highly individual. One gardener's soft and subtle

FACING PAGE: *The pink of lilies and coral bells combines beautifully with silver lamb's ears.*

LEFT: *When blue is added to pink, the result is mauve or lilac, as in this opium poppy, an annual that returns perennially from seed.*

composition may appear insipid to another, while a boisterous bed of hot reds and yellows will leave the lover of pastels cold. For those of us who appreciate all colors, the challenge is to compose our rhapsodies in blue—and yellow, rose, purple and green—while keeping the worst clashes to a minimum.

I've often wondered whether an appreciation for color harmony is innate or learned. Do colors that appear to "go together" do so everywhere at all times? Or does culture teach us to perceive pink and lavender as lovely together and to shy away from orange and magenta in combination? Nature or nurture: the same questions could be asked in musical terms. Is a particular combination of notes heard as harmonious everywhere, or does a chord that rings sweetly on the ear in one place grate on the nerves somewhere else?

Most of us are in the habit of regularly making decisions about color, choices we invest with a fair bit of thought and feeling. Painting the

small entrance room of our house, we went through three colors—actually put paint on the wall, stood back and recoiled at the awfulness of the effect—before settling on a shade we felt comfortable with. It was a lesson learned about proportion: What looked quite pleasant as a small color chip appeared hideous when blown up to wall size. (At least the woman at the hardware store was amused.) Color touches us, stirs us, jars or relaxes us; color is never neutral—even the ubiquitous beige walls of my childhood conveyed a message.

COLOR WORDS

Before we can talk about color in the garden, we need to scan the spectrum and agree on a working vocabulary. The language of color can be confusing—so many shades, so few

agreed-upon terms. Green, gray, white and brown are easy. For the rest, some folks simply distill the discussion down to red, yellow, blue, orange, pink, maybe purple—a fair start but not quite adequate to the task. Planning a garden calls for an idiom both broader and more precise. Simple "yellow" or "blue" does not tell us enough; whether a flower is primrose-yellow or mustard-yellow, sky-blue or lavender-blue may precipitate a change of plan.

Catalogs are not always helpful to the cause of accurate color naming, insisting as they sometimes do on describing magenta as rose-pink or lavender as blue. At the opposite pole are the fussy few who treat the subject of color as an exact science, making subtle distinctions between every shade and charting the process with wheels and scales until you wonder whether you're planting flowers or

picking out wallpaper, bedspread and matching drapes. True, gardening is a kind of exterior decoration, but offending petals are soon fallen and plants far easier to move than couches. In my mind's eye, I have a color spectrum and a corresponding list of terms that may chart a middle course between careless naming and splitting hairs. My suggestions about combinations are bound to be idiosyncratic, but they may serve as a springboard as you envision your own garden.

WHITE AND CREAM

There is no dearth of white flowers for both sun and shade. So numerous are they that planting an all-white bed or garden turns out to be a simple thing to do, little more than narrowing down the candidates and arranging the various shapes and sizes. Hav-

FACING PAGE: *Where various white flowers are assembled, you begin to notice not only subtle gradations of tone but the forms of flowers as well.*

LEFT: *Seeded in from the roadside, mauve musk mallow is light enough in hue to accord with yellow and lavender flowers.*

ing never seen a "white garden," Louise Beebe Wilder, our favorite writer from the early 1900s, anticipated she might find it "bleak in effect, or at the very least monotonous." But after visiting one in Wales, she described the reality as "frank and fresh and full of changing values…neither funereal nor weddingish in appearance." At twilight, "when the hand of man is less apparent and mysterious agencies seem to have brought [the garden] into being," it "was almost as if a mist had crept up from the river and, finding the haven of this quiet enclosure, had swirled around and about, rising here in wraith spires and turrets, lying there in gauzy breadths amidst the muted green—so soft, so ethereal…half real it seemed."

At Larkwhistle, our Quiet Garden is a variation on the white-flower theme: a few shadowy blue clema-

tises have a place, and a quarter of the perennials—various grasses and hostas—contribute the quiet grays and greens of their foliage. Interesting things happen when most of the flowers are white. You begin to notice the diversity of form much more, the different bells and stars, cups, hearts, tiny trumpets, triangles, and so on. You also perceive subtle differences in coloring: the flat paper-white of perennial sweet peas, the skim-milk shade of *Veronicastrum virginicum*'s skinny spires, the greenish white florets of delphiniums and the opal tones in the heart of a peony. And because many white flowers make up for want of color by a waft of fragrance, a sweet air usually hangs over them.

White flowers present a gardener with few obvious dilemmas, acting as they do as neutral highlights and potential buffers between other colors. But curiously, white is not always the unifying color you might imagine. We once added white Shasta daisies to a border decked out in pinks and blues: rugosa roses, Siberian irises, gas plant, painted daisies, peonies, pinks, catmint, and such. When the daisies bloomed, their stark white broke the flow of color as surely as if it had been mustard-yellow. More often, though, the contrast of white adds vivacity to a picture, as the same Shasta daisies would alongside red yarrow or peach daylilies with nearby blue veronica or lavender balloon flowers. White flowers and silver foliage are safe bets with magenta blossoms; and white and yellow together are always fresh and cheerful. Welcome in any setting is the misty white of baby's breath, a haze of tiny blooms floating light and inoffensive wherever the plant takes hold in the sun.

Cream—white tinged with a little yellow—is a useful blender, a color in harmony with all. Would that more flowers wore this gentle hue. In June, cream bearded iris act as useful bridges between the effulgent colors of that month. At the same time, branched plumes of goat's beard (*Aruncus dioicus*) sweep the air like enormous creamy feathers. Three months later, tall *Artemisia lactiflora*—the second name means milky-flowered—creates a similar effect; *A. lactiflora* 'Guizho,' shorter and tidier than its parent, has dark purplish stems below sprays of tiny cream stars; new to us, this iron-hardy perennial is sure to find its way into various groupings. It is worth noting that these cream artemisias, fine with most other colors, look rather dirty in association with pure white.

The flat creamy heads of *Achillea* 'Anthea' fit in anywhere, as do the buff flowers of the yarrow known as 'Great Expectations' (or 'Hoffnung'). August brings the cream torch lily, *Kniphofia* 'Little Maid,' a pale, slender

version of a perennial that is usually hot-colored and robust; like other torch lilies, its small, downturned tubular flowers, arranged in a tapering spire, open in succession over several weeks. Grasses or hostas with foliage striped or splashed with yellow or white also count as cream, and their generous use can only foster harmony.

YELLOW

As I muse over colors and how to combine them, I find it helpful to break yellow into several shades ranging from light to dark. The hedgerow primrose of English springs gives its name to a soft light yellow, a tender hue that (like cream) accords with most others. More intense is lemon-yellow, seen at its prettiest in the indispensable 'Moonshine' yarrow and the old-fashioned

lemon lily (*Hemerocallis flava*). Like its namesake, lemon-yellow is sharp and refreshing, an assertive shade that can either enliven or detract. My preference—and again, all of this is completely subjective—is to see lemon with white and other shades of yellow as well as with blue, lavender and violet but kept clear of most pinks, purples, magentas and even orange. Some lovely sparks fly when lemon gets next to the warm red known as scarlet.

Sometimes unplanned pairings open our eyes to fresh color combinations. In our Yellow Border, light mauve musk mallows (*Malva moschata*) jumped in from the roadside and made themselves at home next to 'Moonshine' yarrow. Lemon and mauve is a match I would never have made but will not unmake. When we used to grow purple loose-strife (now horticulturally incorrect

FACING PAGE: *Pure red glows next to white but may come on too strong for some tastes when teamed with bold yellow or magenta.*

TOP LEFT: *Red bergamot makes a warm picture with the fruit shades of daylilies and a cooler scheme with blue and violet aconite; there is no rule against putting all of them together.*

BOTTOM LEFT: *Strong but complementary describes the color combination of yellow leopard's bane and purple alliums.*

because of its rampant invasion of wetlands), I always enjoyed its deep mauve with lemon Turk's-cap lilies, baby's breath and silver lamb's ears. Grasses and foliage plants with yellowish lights shining through their green are fine with lemon, and as the leaves of 'Moonshine' yarrow demonstrate, lemon works mighty well with silver.

In nature, yellow is the most abundant flower color of all. The round silky petals of the evening primrose (*Oenothera tetragona*, also known as *O. fruticosa* or *O. youngii*) represent yellow in its clearest form. Yellow loosestrife, knapweed, mulleins and a host of summer daisies fall in here too. "Flowers of light," Louise Beebe Wilder calls them, going on to say that "all yellow flowers, like the light of which they seem to be fashioned, blend and combine or flash back at each other with never a jar to the most sensitive eye. They are the sunshine of the garden." And most of them love to grow in the sun. I'm so taken with yellow in association with blue, lavender and silver that I have made a summer border of just these colors (see the chapter "Hot and Dry"). Gardeners yearning for more intensity need only add scarlet to the mix of yellows and watch the fireworks start. There is something passionate about red and yellow together—the words torrid and fiery come to mind—like one of those intense, combative romances held together by strength of character on both sides. Oddly enough, red and yellow both harmonize and contrast, both attract and repel. Judging by May tulip beds, the combination is ever popular.

With a touch of brown, pure yellow deepens to mustard, a shade seen in the yarrow *Achillea filipendulina*

and its cultivars 'Coronation Gold' and 'Gold Plate.' A common enough color—and maybe familiarity has bred a trace of contempt—mustard stands in bold and beautiful contrast with dusky violet (as in the classic border combination of this yarrow with *Salvia* x *superba*) or in gentler harmony with white and the cool lavender-blues of sea holly, campanulas, catmints, and such. Any of the summer lilies or daylilies with honey or brownish undertones get along with mustard. But for my taste, a little mustard goes a long way.

You can also get too much of the acerbic greenish yellow displayed by perennial alyssum and, more sharply, by cushion spurge (*Euphorbia polychroma*), both of which I admire for their early flowering but find hard to work into pictures. Perhaps because its flowers lean more to green than yellow, I have no qualms

about using Lady's mantle (*Alchemilla mollis*) with a broad brush in almost any situation.

RED AND SURROUNDING SHADES

Start adding red to yellow, and you move into all the luscious fruit shades—apricot, peach, melon and finally orange—that add so much warmth and juiciness to a garden. No perennials show off this slice of the spectrum as well as daylilies, with bearded irises not far behind. Geums, herbaceous potentillas, mulleins, foxtail lilies, true lilies, torch lilies, crocosmia and some poppies also contribute to the fruit bowl. Lovely close harmonies, almost mouthwatering in their richness, result when these colors are gathered together with white, lavender, sky-blue, palest blush-pink (as in climbing rose 'New Dawn') and

deeper tones of scarlet, wine and violet. To my eye, lemon looks harsh in this context, and mustard comes across as muddy. Virtually all of the fruit colors bicker incessantly with the mauves and magentas so common among perennials, an argument you're bound to hear every July and August when lilies and daylilies flirt with geraniums, phloxes, rose campion and hollyhocks. Referee, please.

Red, like blue, is a word much bandied about in reference to flowers of quite different colors. Relatively few wear true red, which I think of as the color of red bergamot, *Monarda* 'Cambridge Scarlet.' That cultivar name is not strictly accurate, scarlet being a warm red with a dab of yellow in it, as seen in scarlet lychnis (*Lychnis chalcedonica*).

Increase the yellow in red, and you're heading back to orange. Add blue to red, and you move in the

FACING PAGE: *Pink pinks and lavender bellflowers typify a color match that most people find harmonious.*

LEFT: *This Asiatic lily shows the cooler (or bluer) side of pink, as opposed to salmon, which is warm pink, with a hint of orange in it.*

other direction, toward crimson, a cool red seen in some peonies and roses. This, for me, is the dividing line between warm and cool colors. Pure red stands in the middle. Red bergamot, for example, works equally well with burnished (warm) daylilies or blue (cool) monkshood. On one side, warm scarlet-reds blend best with yellows, the fruit shades, white and lavender. On the other side, cool crimson-red harmonizes with blue, rose, mauve and magenta. The very few wine-red flowers—velvety sweet

William, dark daylilies, some lilies, clematis, hollyhocks and maroon-leafed shrubs and perennials—I enjoy anywhere; their shadowy quality adds depth and resonance (a bass line) to the rest.

PINK

Keep adding white to red, and you arrive at pink. But the pink you get depends on the red you start with. Pink on the warm side—that is, with underlying yellow—may be thought

ture—something we're loath to do because the clumps are thriving—and the peony perks right up.

BLUE

Everybody likes blue. But I wonder how many gardeners have planted some perennial hoping for heavenly blue only to end up with lavender? Plant vendors are notorious for pawning off half-related shades as blue, and you soon learn to take a catalog's blue promises with a grain of salt. Blue flowers are not in short supply, but there are surely fewer of them than there are of lavender, a color that inspires far less enthusiasm. For true blue, look to the family Boraginaceae, a treasure trove of amethyst, sapphire, turquoise, azure, cerulean. Here you'll find forget-me-nots, Virginia bluebells and lungworts in spring. June brings the big blue Italian bugloss (*Anchusa azurea*) and the rare blue comfrey—a plant we have seen in other gardens but never in our own, despite buying what turned out to be impostors several times. Look also to delphiniums, best of blue flowers, from sky to navy and every blue between, and get them next to climbing roses for glorious effects.

Rock gardeners doting on blue soon light on gentians, while certain spiderworts—*Tradescantia* 'Zwanenburg Blue' and 'Blue Stone'—bring this favored color to rough corners in shade. More true blue is found among spring hyacinths, perennial flax (*Linum perenne*), irises both bearded and Siberian, perennial cornflower, Jacob's ladder, sea holly, veronicas and monkshood, not to mention the celestial Himalayan blue poppy. As I see it, blue can do no wrong in matters of associations. Put it with yellow, apricot, buff and peach; put it with pink warm or cool; next to red is fine; it's lovely with white, mauve, magenta and silver. Wherever blue appears, it seems to grace the place and chime along in harmony.

of as salmon. Pink Oriental poppies (and gorgeous is their flaunting crêpe) are invariably salmon, bred from marrying the original scarlet-orange species with white. Salmon bumped up with orange becomes the strange strong hue of tiger lilies.

If the starting red is crimson, lightening it with white leads to rose-pink, that cool sweet color found in so many old-fashioned roses and one of the loveliest floral dyes. When I use the word pink, my inner eye sees 'Queen of Denmark' roses. Why this

color has come to be associated with all things tender and dear, with love and emotions of the heart, I cannot say; nor can I say why crimson is so sensual and scarlet so sexy.

Like many close relatives, salmon-pink and rose-pink tend to squabble. If you don't believe me, plant a salmon Oriental poppy beside a cool pink peony. We did. Poppy outshines peony because the poppy's yellow lights, felt if not seen, make the peony's lavender undertones look drab. Remove poppies from the pic-

FACING PAGE: *The vibrant magenta of phlox can be discordant, but it is well matched with annual lavatera 'Silver Cup' and the neutral gray and tan of sea lyme grass.*

LEFT: *Mauve mallows and big blue anchusa seed themselves in Larkwhistle's Kitchen Garden, where they enhance lilac widow's tears (tradescantia) and airy white crambe.*

LAVENDER

The scented flower spikes of a lavender bush give us the color's name. Lavender is blue's quiet cousin, soft-spoken and a bit melancholy—blue with the lights dimmed. And dim it was once called—"bleak blue," a "sad hue." I would call it overlooked, the color most consistently passed by without notice in our garden. There is nothing flashy or sensational about lavender, but its very quietude makes it an ideal blender.

As one color-sensitive gardener noted, lavender "seems to have no edges, but a melting…quality like the blue of the distance." Next to lavender, even "combative red loses much of its truculence and becomes a softened thing."

Lavender's salient feature is the absence of any tinge of red. Whether pale verging on gray or deepened to the point of violet, it matters little. Light or dark, lavender is a cool pacific shade that fits comfortably in any color scheme, flatters adjacent

hues, draws discordant elements together and helps calm a riot of color. The gardener's unassuming friend, lavender lends a sense of repose and dignity to any planting. My only caveat would be that next to bright-eyed true blue, lavender's underlying grayness is more apparent; otherwise, I'd put it anywhere. The same holds true for pure violet, the color of sweet violets (*Viola odorata*) blooming in spring lawns and of the well-known Jackman's clematis. Violet is lavender taken to shadowy depths, and there is no perennial pairing that this sumptuous dark color does not enhance. Too bad there isn't more of it around.

Lavender flowers span the seasons, from spring's creeping phlox until the light goes out of the last perennial aster in late fall. In between come vinca, catmints in several shapes and sizes (*Nepeta* spp), var-

ious columbines and salvias, many irises, a bevy of bellflowers (*Campanula* spp), the dark balloon flower, globe thistles, some clematis, Russian sage, hosta flowers, sea lavender and a few hardy geraniums—lots of lavender for sun or shade.

MAUVE AND MAGENTA

As soon as lavender gets mixed up with red, we enter the vast realm of mauve, magenta and purple—shades that the gods most definitely favor. Garden writer Thalassa Cruso says that in her family, washed-out magenta—the original color of wild sweet peas, phlox, petunias, foxgloves, and many more—was called Garden-of-Eden, on the assumption that all flowers must surely have been dyed that way in the beginning. Divine bias has not kept a century of garden commentators from heaping

scorn on "malignant magenta." Even otherwise sympathetic writers talk of "that awful form of floral original sin, magenta." It looks to me, though, as if the tide of disapproval is shifting. In our garden it has. If you can't beat magenta, we figure, you might as well welcome it and do a little match-making.

Mauve is rose-pink leaning toward lavender, the shade of those roadside musk mallows. A cordial color, it shies away only from scarlet, the fruit shades, mustard-yellow and salmon, all of which make mauve look cloudy by comparison. As mauve deepens to magenta (purple loosestrife stands magenta proud and pure), the same warnings hold. Warm reds, oranges and yellows bring out the worst in magenta, turning what might be a pleasant hue into something crabby and dour. Example: next to scarlet sweet William, magenta foxgloves

appear dull and faded; the same foxgloves turn into spires of glory when matched with deep crimson peonies, lavender bellflowers and silver artemisia. The intensely magenta rose campion (*Lychnis coronaria*) likes to taunt by showing up next to apricot daylilies; far be it from me to interfere. But given our druthers, we'd put this shocking biennial among blue monkshood, white baby's breath or mauve phlox. Washed-out shades of magenta give the color a bad name. Try as I may, I can't bring myself to like the faded flowers of the *Spiraea* 'Anthony Waterer'; worse yet is its yellowleafed version.

No family of perennials wears mauve and magenta as flauntingly as hardy geraniums. The shallow saucers of *Geranium sanguineum*— long-lived, long-blooming and carefree—are unalloyed magenta. In our garden, it grows among bluish Siberian irises, metallic sea hollies, lavender catmint and violet *Viola cornuta* in a border backed by pink rugosa roses. If an orange California poppy lodges in this bed, we simply pull it out—they have the run of the rest of the garden and better not complain. Many summer phloxes, too, deal in shades of magenta, and again, we have recourse to blues, mauve-

pinks, white and silver for company.

One of the most enjoyable aspects of gardening, color-scheming adds another dimension to the whole endeavor—a sense of creative play. As soon as you start thinking in terms of color associations and picture-making, your imagination leaps into action. A patch of earth becomes a canvas, a place to work out your horticultural visions. The garden, of course, has a life of its own. Winter messes things up and leaves gaps (which become opportunities for trying new plants). Stray seedlings spring up, accidental colors that either delight with their rightness or annoy the heck out of you and dare you to erase them. The important thing, though, is that the garden be a place of refreshment and recreation, that it bear the impression of your hands and heart. As John Sedding, English garden writer of the last century, said: "A garden is preeminently a place to indulge individual taste . . . let me say that the best general rule

that I can devise for garden-making is: Put all the beauty and delightsomeness you can into your garden, get all the beauty and delight you can out of your garden, never minding a little mad want of balance, and think of the proprieties afterward."

FACING PAGE: *In September, Japanese anemones accord with fall asters in a close color match.*

TOP LEFT: *The lavender of the milky bellflower and many other campanulas works well in any setting.*

BOTTOM LEFT: *The hot magenta-pink of Geranium psilostemon is a hard color to companion; blue and white neighbors are safe bets.*

The Art of Perennial Gardening

FADE OUT, FADE IN

SPRING BULBS WITH SUMMER PERENNIALS

*"As soon as spring is in the air,
Mr. Krippendorf and I begin an
antiphonal chorus, like two
frogs in neighboring ponds:
What have you in bloom…"*

ELIZABETH LAWRENCE

FACING PAGE: *Fall-planted bulbs bring
welcome spring color to Larkwhistle's
Old Garden, where they are succeeded
by a host of later perennials.*

ABOVE: *Reticulata irises and snow
crocuses belong together in the sun.*

A PERENNIAL GARDEN BEGINS TO SHOW sparks of color the moment winter softens into spring, weeks before most annuals would have a hope of living through a night. How welcome are the flocks of crocuses, daffodils, scillas, grape hyacinths and tulips. There are no stand-ins for the flowers that spring up from fall-planted bulbs; for April and May, the choice is largely between bulbs and bare ground. But bulbs can be a nuisance in a perennial bed. They get in the way; or more to the point, they are too far out of the way, hidden underground, just when you need to see them. Out of sight, out of mind. At times, even the most organized gardener is hard-pressed to remember where bulbs are taking their rest. Inevitably, the awful moment comes during fall renovations or spring digging when—slice, stab—metal meets bulb.

The other problem with bulbs, of course, is the messy aftermath they leave in their wake. As sure as summer follows spring, blossoms give way to withering yellow leaves and, finally, to a gaping blank.

It's tempting to leave bulbs out of perennial plantings altogether or give them a bed of their own. Better yet, a special spring garden like the one English gardener Vita Sackville-West made at Sissinghurst: You come through the gate, turn a corner, and suddenly you're in a magical flower-filled "room," all the lovelier in contrast with the prevailing brown-and-green outside. A pretty plan, to be sure (and possible if you have lots of land and help), but most of us need to find practical ways to bring bulbs and perennials together in the same space.

Over the years at Larkwhistle, we've devised methods of growing spring bulbs among summer perennials. In April and May, borders are alight with flowers, but by mid-June, a different scene is unfolding, and evidence of what has been is largely hidden. Bulbs fade out; perennials fade in. The trick is accomplished by associating spring bulbs with summer perennials that grow up to cover dying bulb leaves with their own fresh foliage. But not every perennial is a suitable cover. An important piece of the puzzle involves choosing perennials that can stay in place for many years without the need for division or replacement. The less you fuss with their companion plants, the less risk you run of damaging bulbs. Because bulbs come in all sizes, from the slightest snowdrops to tall tulips, meshing them with perennials takes some care. But when the garden wakes up perky and colorful in spring, you're glad you made the effort.

FACING PAGE: *It takes some planning to mesh spring flowers with summer perennials, but it is an exercise well worth undertaking.*

LEFT: *Strong-growing border plants such as arabis, catmint, cerastium and dianthus (seen here) can withstand the competition of crocuses growing through or near them.*

SMALL AND EARLY

Snowdrops (*Galanthus elwesii* and *G. nivalis*) are among the first bulbs to appear. Unlike crocuses, the small white flowers can look out of place at the front of a straight-edged border, even though their stature points to such a site. There is something shy in them—a touch of wildness—that wants a more naturalistic setting. Snowdrops like a little shade too— the dappling of nearby shrubs or small trees starting to leaf out.

Making a virtue of necessity, we give snowdrops a picturesque setting while providing them with the conditions they need.

At the back of our Quiet Garden is an area shaded by tall lilacs. At their base is spread a carpet of ground covers and shade plants: delicate sweet woodruff (*Asperula odorata*, or *Galium odoratum*), with thin-fingered leaves and tiny white flowers; green-and-silver lamium (*Lamium maculatum* 'Album'), with short spikes of hooded white flowers; and a white version of

glossy green vinca, sometimes called myrtle or periwinkle. With the ground covers are five clumps of hosta 'Francis Williams,' its gray-green leaves edged with cream. And pushing into the lilac's lower branches is a colony of Solomon's seal (*Polygonatum multiflorum*). Matched in vigor, these plants bloom in turn, and all keep their leaves into fall. Directly through them were planted several hundred snowdrop bulbs stolen from other parts of the garden. Every April, while the ground covers are rousing themselves and the hostas are still sleeping in, the snowdrops do their dainty thing. In a few weeks, their ripening foliage is obscured by fresh growth and other flowers.

To this same scene—a departure from the green-and-white theme—could be added the blue notes of scillas, small spring bulbs that thrive in

shade. Overlapping with snowdrops, the first of the scillas, the tongue-twisting *Scilla mischtschenkoana* (once known as *S. tubergeniana*), brings short spikes of pale blue star flowers; the common dark blue scilla (*S. siberica*) would also do nicely. Both bulbs are easy, hardy and quick to multiply.

An ideal addition to such a shady spring bed is the foot-tall (30 cm) snakeshead fritillary, or guinea-hen flower (*Fritillaria meleagris*). The first name comes from the Latin *fritillus*, meaning dice box. Nodding and boxy, the flowers are dusky purple or white, checkered with a grid of fine lines like the plumage of a guinea fowl. This unusual spring bulb opens after the snowdrops, then its slender leaves fade tidily away.

If the lilacs hadn't been here, we might have considered native service-berries to give shade and shelter. Both

Amelanchier alnifolia and *A. canadensis* bloom early, a flurry of small five-petaled white flowers interspersed with pale bronze leaves. Also known as shadbush, shadblow and Juneberry, these hardy shrubs ripen purple pea-sized fruit that is good to eat but time-consuming to pick. Birds will harvest any fruit you miss (or—more likely—the other way around). Two or three serviceberry bushes planted 4 to 6 feet (1.2 to 1.8 m) apart form a shrubby umbrella over an assembly of bulbs and attendant ground covers.

Colonies of snowdrops and other early bulbs are striking against the wine stems of red osier dogwood (*Cornus alba*) or the green stems of kerria (*Kerria japonica* 'Pleniflora'), which produces fluffy yellow flowers in June. A pruning tip: Rather than chopping such shrubs into awkward shapes—boxes, balls, cones—cut

FACING PAGE: *Catmint (foreground), daylilies and irises will soon rise up to mask the messy aftermath of spring bulbs.*

LEFT: *A smaller variety, crocus 'Whitwell Purple,' poses no threat to the mat of arabis growing over its bulbs.*

some of the oldest stems back to the ground from time to time; this opens the bushes, contains their growth and allows them to assume a natural form.

Other shrubs associate well with small bulbs and shade-tolerant perennials. The elegant magnolias, both star (*Magnolia stellata*) and saucer (*M.* x *soulangiana*), throw light shade. The same can be said of well-pruned crabapples, flowering cherries and pears. What could be prettier than a budding magnolia or cherry above a blue-and-white quilt of snowdrops and scillas? Small early daffodils such as 'Tête-à-Tête' interspersed here and there add sunny yellow to an otherwise cool picture.

Known as understory plants, serviceberries, dogwoods and magnolias grow naturally in woodlands in the shade of taller trees. As such, they are ideal for both the front and back gardens of city homes where buildings and grand old street trees throw long shadows for part of the day. Red-stemmed dogwoods (as opposed to flowering dogwoods), serviceberries, crabapples and flowering pears are hardy in areas colder than zone 5; magnolias, cherries and kerria are usually not.

TWO FOR THE SUN

Out in the sun, the first irises, wee *Iris reticulata* and its hybrids, put on a brave show as snow crocuses come into bloom. By snow crocuses, I mean both the original species (as found in nature) and a handful of varieties bred from them, all smaller and earlier than the fat Dutch hybrids. Contrasting beautifully in color and form, reticulata irises and snow crocuses belong together. Most fall bulb catalogs list both, and the matchmaking possibilities are intriguing. The reddish purple of *Iris reticulata* 'J.S. Dijt' is echoed by the neat purple strokes on the white petals of crocus 'Lady Killer.' A favorite combination is light blue iris 'Cantab' with crocus 'Cream Beauty.' A bolder picture teams deep violet (and violet-scented) *Iris reticulata*, the original species, with vivid orange *Crocus ancyrensis*. Silvery lavender *Crocus tommasinianus* highlights dark violet iris 'Springtime.' Nothing is sprightlier at the edge of a perennial bed in April than bunches of the strong-growing blue reticulata iris 'Harmony' popping through a mixed band of cream, yellow, orange and white snow crocuses. Dwarf daylilies planted along the

son'— or some of the smaller hardy geraniums would accomplish the cover-up.

CROCUSES AND COVER

Before spring is too far along, just when our eyes are yearning for swaths of definite color, the big Dutch crocuses pop their buds in sunnier parts of the garden. At Larkwhistle, these cheerful, easy flowers—bouquets of purple, lavender, white and orange—flow along the front of beds in association with later perennials. Because the increasing crocus corms eventually sprout dense bundles of leaves, we match them with perennials able to compete. In some spots, crocuses come up directly through edging plants.

Double arabis (*Arabis albida*, or *A. caucasica*, 'Flore Plena'), one of our best front-row plants, is underplanted with plum-purple and lavender-striped crocuses to form a picture that has reprised every April for more than a decade with little attention. Pretty against the mat of gray arabis leaves, the crocuses are also protected from spattering mud and (so far) from foraging mice and squirrels. As arabis comes into flower, crocus leaves are lost to sight. Across the path, a patch of ordinary snow-in-summer (*Cerastium tomentosum*) looks the worse for wear after a winter under soggy snow, but yellow and white crocuses bloom thickly through it. Soon the cerastium rebounds to take over the space (and then some, if we're lax about controlling it) with silver leaves and white June flowers.

If suitable edging plants are already established, plant crocuses right through them—simply dig in with a narrow trowel, or poke a hole with the trowel handle or special dibber and push in a corm. This is called underplanting. When starting from scratch, set the edging perennials a foot (30 cm) apart—five arabis will

same edge will obliterate all traces of fading bulb leaves in a few weeks.

Standing all of 6 inches (15 cm) high, reticulata irises top snow crocuses by a finger or two. Set the irises in a gently curving two- or three-ply band with crocuses in front and flowing back into the irises here and there. Since both acquit themselves well in light loam and full sun, they are right for a rock-garden slope or the front of a flowerbed where later-blooming perennials wait in the wings to take over. Fronting one of

our beds, nine plants of coral bells display their marbled leaves and pink blooms for many weeks in summer. In among the coral bells, we've poked a few dozen 'Cream Beauty' crocus and behind them some blue reticulata irises. The crocus leaves are so small, they are soon overgrown by the coral bells. When half-ripened, the tall, thin iris foliage is gently bent over, pressed to the ground and tucked under the foliage of nearby plants. In place of coral bells, a low sedum—'Ruby Glow' or 'Vera Jame-

run together to form a good big patch—and plant crocuses between.

Down the way, crocuses are planted between clumps of ornamental catmint (*Nepeta* x *faassenii* or *N.* 'Blue Beauty,' also known as 'Souvenir d'André Chaudron'), vigorous perennials that billow into gray-green mounds decorated with lavender-blue spikes from June onward. In April, crocuses brighten ground that would otherwise be bare; the bulbs are snugged right up to the catmint—this is called interplanting—

which eventually spills over their yellowing leaves. One catmint will cover for a couple of dozen crocuses. Three catmints set two hand spans apart fill a 5-foot (1.5 m) stretch, making possible a massed crocus planting.

The same fade-out, fade-in magic happens where crocuses are planted among perennials that die back to a tight crown each winter and regrow strongly every summer. Some of the best for the purpose are Lady's mantle (*Alchemilla mollis*), *Artemisia* 'Silver

The Art of Perennial Gardening

Mound,' *Geranium sanguineum* and the tumbling dwarf baby's breath called *Gypsophila* 'Rosy Veil,' as well as shorter ornamental grasses and smaller daylilies suitable for the front row. Planting crocus corms among front-row perennials, even those already in place for years, is a sure, quick way to squeeze in an extra season of color. But be warned: Thick sods of crocus leaves soon overshadow creeping thymes, choke out creeping phlox, smother dianthus and generally wreak havoc among smaller perennials. Believe me, I've seen it—and probably recommended the combinations before I learned better.

When crocuses are in bloom, there are precious few flowering shrubs or trees to lift the color from ground level. One exception is the ubiquitous forsythia, a shrub much more appealing when allowed to assume a naturally graceful shape. Yes, it grows out of bounds, but is that any reason to hack the poor thing into some weird cubist form? Position it carefully, then let forsythia be its fountainlike self, arching yellow-wreathed boughs over a floor of white, purple and lavender crocuses. See if you're not happier with it that way. Another early shrub, the bright coral Japanese quince (*Chaenomeles speciosa*), like small single roses, makes a striking picture with dark purple crocuses at its feet.

SPRING PINK

The daphnes are a group of smaller shrubs, most wonderfully fragrant, some wearing decorative silver- or gold-edged leaves. First to flower and perfectly hardy here is *Daphne mezereum*, called the Mezereon in older books. At an improbably early date, before any sign of leaves, the 3-foot (1 m) bush wraps itself in a flowery wine-purple scarf heavily doused with scent. Below it blooms a carpet of mauve *Bulbocodium vernum*, the so-called meadow saffron, a seldom-seen spring bulb that holds its narrow petals close to the ground. Repeating the color, but a few shades lighter, is pale pink glory-of-the-snow (*Chionodoxa luciliae* 'Pink Giant'), not too giant at 8 inches (20 cm). A deeper note comes from crocus 'Whitwell Purple,' a small bulb quick to increase. Daphne wants a sheltered site in soil enriched with well-rotted leaves or other organic matter, both in the soil and as a top mulch; an annual handful of lime where the soil tends to acidity may help.

Several summer perennials continue the pink-and-purple scheme and keep the space in foliage and

flower after the bulbs. At the front, set three or more plants of the dwarf hardy geranium 'Ballerina,' a treasure worth searching for. Spreading to dinner-plate diameter, it shows a succession of light pink saucers veined with maroon above lobed leaves that become streaked with red in fall. The small geraniums should be placed 1 foot (30 cm) apart.

In the next row, at a distance of 18 inches (45 cm), try *Heuchera diversifolia* (or *H. micrantha*) 'Palace Purple,' with handsomely pleated burgundy leaves and wiry stems set with tiny white flowers; an alternative would be 'Palace Passion,' with smaller leaves and light pink blooms. If you can afford the hefty price tag and are willing to gamble on its survival, the plum-purple Lenten rose (*Helleborus orientalis*), a foot tall (30 cm) and early-flowering, belongs here. For height and variety where space allows, use fanning astilbes, hostas or Siberian irises in the background. Tuck the small bulbs mentioned above between the shorter perennials and use narcissus—I like the early white 'Thalia,' with its clustered flowers like birds on the wing—between the taller perennials. Leave a narrow band around each perennial free of bulbs. The tapestry of bulbs flowers first, followed by a concealing curtain of fresh foliage and bloom.

DAYS OF DAFFODILS

When it comes to daffodils, I echo the sentiment of one of our mentors-through-books, Louise Beebe Wilder: It would ill become me (as she would say) to speak about these light-filled flowers from the standpoint of a dispassionate expert; instead, I approach them as an admirer, full of enthusiasm, willing to overlook their few shortcomings.

Driving through the country in spring or wandering around city side streets gawking into people's yards, I'm always surprised at how few daffodils are grown. Most gardens have a clump or two of big yellow trumpets—end of story. Which is too bad, because daffodils decorate a garden with an unmatched freshness, and yellow is just the start. In our garden, daffodils take center stage for about six weeks, from cool April days when little 'Tête-à-Tête' and the taller 'February Gold' appear until fragrant poet's narcissus and jonquils wrap up toward the end of May.

Shortcomings? As befits their diva

status, daffodils (once the bloom is off) go through a drawn-out demise, their slowly fading leaves lying around limp and indecorous for so long that you want to shout "Die, already!" But a plant's first priority is survival—ripening foliage feeds next year's flowering—and to heck with our idea of aesthetics. Even a dozen daffodils send up so many leaves that it's hard to ignore their exit.

At Larkwhistle, we get around the problem of fading foliage and ensuing bare patches in the usual way: teaming daffodils with later-blooming perennials that will raise a green screen over them as they wither. And lately, we have also taken to naturalizing surplus bulbs in an old orchard, where they ripen unhindered and unnoticed in the tall grass. Let's have a look at the two approaches.

Most daffodils—the classic trumpets, those with large or small cups

and doubles—reach 18 to 24 inches (45 to 60 cm), with a few taller yet, a stature appropriate to the middle sections of a bed. And as the tallest flowers of their season, they also show up well near the back. These are precisely the places where bulkier summer perennials—potential screens—are beginning to break through. Here is a chance to have your daffodils and hide them too. As a rule, we plant perennials in groups of three or more of a kind. One approach is to weave daffodil bulbs *through* such a group, bulbs and perennials occupying more or less the same area. Another way is to plant bulbs in a band, two or three bulbs wide, sandwiched *between* groups of two different perennials. In both cases, the perennials are set a little farther apart to make room for bulbs but close enough that their leaves meet in a canopy over the daffodils as they die back.

Some examples: An exciting recent addition to our garden is a lovely meadow rue (*Thalictrum aquilegifolium*); its last name tells you it has foliage like an aquilegia (columbine), fan-shaped and light grayish green. Both dainty and stately, this hardy 4-foot (1.2 m) European sends up strong leafy stems that break into sprays of fluffy rosy lilac bloom. Three or more plants, set a full 2 feet (60 cm) apart at the back of a bed, create a hazy, out-of-focus effect in mid-June, a light counterpoint to peonies, pink or crimson painted daisies and blue Siberian irises. Among the thalictrum, there is room for a dozen daffodil bulbs planted about 8 inches (20 cm) apart, with no bulbs coming within a hand span of the perennials. The thalictrum comes up literally like an umbrella—straight stems and overarching leaves—through the *passé* daf-

FACING PAGE: *Before too long, daylilies, phlox and aconite will draw a green and flowery curtain over the yellowing leaves of tulips and narcissus.*

LEFT: *The little star of Bethlehem will soon be hidden under hosta leaves.*

fodils. Both bulbs and meadow rue are good for many years, possibly a decade or more. This duo does well in sun, even better in dappled shade, in soil top-dressed with leaf mold or compost every fall.

In even shadier spots, sweet Cicely (*Myrrhis odorata*) fills in for meadow rue with ferny leaves that form a complete cover over earlier daffodils. Its flat off-white flowerheads, like rounds of old lace, bloom in early summer. Tasting of licorice, sweet Cicely leaves—with the addition of mint and lemon balm—brew a delicious herb tea fresh from the garden; its unripe green seeds are a delicious nibble. This is a bulky plant, a filler that takes up a lot of room and seeds itself to boot; but nothing is quite as enduring in partial shade. When sweet Cicely starts to look tatty in July, cut it back almost to the ground for a fresh start.

Goat's beard (*Aruncus dioicus*) grows a grand canopy of handsome leaves that last all season. In early summer, its creamy plumes wave like a giant astilbe in the air for a week or two before fading too quickly to rust. Sun or light shade, dry soil or damp will suit goat's beard equally well. Occupying a 3-foot-diameter (1 m) space above ground, a single plant conceals a dozen daffodils planted around it.

At 2 to 3 feet (60 to 90 cm) tall, astilbes also cover for daffodils. For best effect, set plants 3 feet (1 m) apart, a generous spacing that allows their beautiful leaves to spread out naturally. We like to pull this tallish perennial toward the front of a bed, the better to appreciate both the pink, white or red plumes and the foliage that stays fresh into fall. Astilbes revel in moist ground and dappled shade; if the earth is damp

enough, they will also do fine in sun.

Siberian irises, graceful relatives of bearded irises, sprout a sheaf of long straight leaves as decorative as many ornamental grasses and perfect camouflage for the similar foliage of daffodils. Three plants set in a vague triangle with 2¹/₂ feet (75 cm) between them leave enough ground for a dozen daffodils scattered around; both are planted in September. A bonus: The Siberian iris clumps stay green and respectable until the going gets quite rough and are the very last perennial to be cut back.

Daylilies, too, grow lots of long, narrow leaves that soon obliterate any signs of daffodils between them. We have a long "catchall" border backed by mixed shrubbery—honeysuckle, mock orange, pussy willow, lilacs, and such—that screens our garden from the road. Here, clumps of assorted daylilies return

strongly every year. Between them runs a ribbon of daffodils that brings the border to life in spring. I would venture to say that daylilies and daffodils are the perfect fade-out, fade-in combination.

A walk around the perennial beds in early May reveals daffodils in bloom among other summer perennials just starting to grow: snakeroot (*Cimicifuga* spp), tall summer phlox, milky mugwort (*Artemisia lactiflora*), spiderwort (*Tradescantia* x *andersoniana*), redhot pokers (*Kniphofia* spp), Siberian catmint (*Nepeta sibirica*) and peonies. In every case, we've chosen perennials that stay in place for many years. When the time comes to lift and divide the perennials, the daffodils, too, will be crowded and ready for renewal.

Wherever daffodils grow among perennials, we routinely bend the bulb leaves over while they are still

green and "comb" them with our fingers in one direction; the foliage of very large clumps is parted like hair, half to one side and half to the other. The object is to get the daffodil leaves as close to the ground as possible and tucked under the foliage of nearby perennials. Bent over and laid low, daffodils apparently suffer no setback in the ripening process; any we treat this way come back each year and continue to multiply.

As lovely as daffodils are on their own, they are even better in company with other bulbs and herbaceous plants of the season. The celestial turquoise of Virginia bluebells (*Mertensia virginica*) belongs with all daffodils, especially those in partial shade, where primroses are also possible. The great orange or yellow bells of tall crown imperials (*Fritillaria imperialis*) are classic company behind daffodils in the sun. Early tulips make possible a number of pictures with the addition of spring border plants such as arabis, aubrieta and creeping phlox in their white, lavender and purple finery. Grape hyacinths (varieties of *Muscari*) pool beautifully blue among the bouquets of white, cream-yellow and orange. Ah, spring!

NATURALIZING NARCISSUS

Part of the landscape left over from the farmstead that has become our garden is an old orchard, an open grassy area watched over by several gnarled apple trees. For years, we ignored the space. Then one September day, in the course of renovating a perennial bed, we unearthed 10-year-old clumps of daffodils so thickly matted it was a wonder they bloomed. Now the first rule of perennial renewal is: Never put back everything you've just taken out—it defeats the purpose. What to do with all those extra bulbs? The old orchard beckoned. Pails full and our imaginations spinning out visions of hosts of daffodils dancing through the grass under apple boughs—we'd seen as much in every English gardening book and in real life one April day at Monet's Giverny in France—we headed into the orchard.

Two slices of a shovel cut away a chunky wedge of sod, leaving a hole deep and wide enough for a couple or three daffodil bulbs snugged into the bottom. After shaking the earth from the sod back into the hole over the bulbs, we topped up with a trowel or two of compost where necessary. We didn't exactly fling the bulbs around and plant where they landed—a method often recommended to free a strict hand from regimentation—but we were careful to avoid anything resembling symmetry, regular spacing or rows. Instead, we roughly delineated broad curving areas where the bulbs were to go and left wide unplanted "pathways" between. In a

few hours, we were patting the soil over the last bulbs—and hoping there would be something to show for the experiment next spring. And sure enough, a May morning dawns, and the easterly sun catches the petals of hundreds of daffodils transforming the rough old orchard with new light.

Beginning in spring, the grassy paths are mowed as needed, but the flowery stretches are left uncut until the daffodil foliage, unnoticed in the tall grass, has withered away. That's the hardest part—the only work, really—pushing the mower through what amounts to hay. Naturalizing daffodils has this going for it: The effort is minimal, the effect glorious. How often can you say that in the garden? But you do need space; naturalizing bulbs in a city lawn is probably pushing it, but wherever there is a stretch of grass—perhaps near the boundaries of a property where shrubs are growing—that can go uncut until midsummer, there is

room for daffodils. Every spring, more flowers sway under the apple trees, and if the daffodil-strewn yard of an untended farm nearby is any indication, that old orchard will be blooming long after we're " 'neath the sod."

FACING PAGE: Where daffodils are planted in the grass, the effect is glorious and the work—except for mowing—minimal.

LEFT: Half-grown geraniums not only provide a leafy setting for daffodils but effectively hide withering bulb foliage later on as well.

UNDER THE LILACS

SPRING FLOWERS IN SHADE

"Even one large tree may invite a kind of woodland gardening in its vicinity."

CHRISTOPHER LLOYD

FACING PAGE: *Showy drumstick primulas and yellow polyanthus typify the colors we welcome in spring.*

ABOVE: *Spring flowers share space with hostas and ferns for later display.*

IT's LATE MARCH. AS WINTER TURNS toward spring, I begin to feel a rising sense of excitement tinged with worry, the kind of feeling you get before setting off on a long trip. The garden itself is familiar enough territory, but each new season holds surprises. During the first few tours around the muddy paths, we're looking as much for winter damage as evidence of growth. Every year, there are a few casualties—a wrecked rose or snow-smashed shrub, vole tunnels where tulip bulbs should have been, a few winter-killed perennials.

But if some hopes are dashed, most are fulfilled. The primroses look a bit ragged, but in their green hearts are points of purple and yellow. Planted last fall, a new meadow rue has survived and is sprouting strongly. Mice have overlooked our favorite wild crocuses. Often, winter damage turns out to be less serious than we had

first thought. On closer inspection, the roses do not look quite as bad; green wood—enough for a fresh start—shows below blackened stems. Fetch the pruning shears. Another season has begun.

I once had a calendar of moon phases, planting dates and pithy advice. Tellingly, the thought (more of a warning) for May was: "Too busy; externals take over." Spring is always hectic, but there is no point letting the rush of work overshadow the reason for doing it. Most perennials have a couple or three weeks of glory; either you take time to enjoy them while they are out, or you miss them altogether. However harried I am with tasks, the first flowers, delicate flakes of color staining earth that last week was frost-bound and bleak, always stop me in my tracks.

Spring is the time I feel the least critical of the garden. Probably

because it's so good to be outside poking around again, flowers are almost a bonus. Still, refinements are possible. As you compose a spring scene, keep in mind three things: a suitable setting for plants, congenial company and pleasing proportions. Early perennials dotted around at random with lots of bare ground between are less effective than a concentrated display. Sometimes, the best plan may be to fill a special bed with spring flowers and drink in the color when you need it most. A bit of drab-and-shabby later on is a small price to pay (and there are ways around that).

SPRING SHADE

In early spring, woodland flowers respond to the warming sun as it filters through bare branches overhead. In the garden, too, certain perennials hurry into flower before the boughs

FACING PAGE: *Japanese bog primroses thrive in light shade and damp ground, even on the banks of a stream.*

LEFT: *Where our spring border veers into the sun, heather bushes and 'Thalia' daffodils continue the color.*

above them break into leaf. A spring border on the shady side of trees or shrubbery can be one of the garden's most appealing features. By way of illustrating the possibilities, let's take a closer look at such a planting at Larkwhistle.

Carved from a flat open hayfield, most of our garden catches the sun all day. But to one side stands a thicket of tall white lilacs, remnant of the old farm, left for decades to sucker and spread. The space beneath them is sunny until late morning; in the afternoon, the lilacs cast long shadows. How could we resist: shade and a ready-made backdrop, a place for a planting quite different from the rest of the garden. Our thoughts turned first to primroses and then to a whole class of early-blooming woodlanders from home and away.

A straight border would have made no sense under the lilacs. Instead, we dug a gently curving strip of ground about 5 feet (1.5 m) wide, its outline roughly corresponding to the natural contours of the shrubs. In

order to nourish the light loam, we then added a few inches of old manure and sifted compost along with a dusting of bone meal. Primroses went in the first year, other perennials the next. Changes were made: plants divided, added, moved, removed. Over the seasons, the border has evolved into a spring scene—a tapestry of mauve, yellow, white and blue—that gladdens the senses after a long winter.

A PROMISE OF PRIMROSES

The season opens in this border with the glorious flowering of the drumstick primrose (*Primula denticulata*). The Latin surname, having the same root (so to speak) as "dentist" and "dental," describes the notched, toothed or in*dent*ed edges of each floret. Drumstick identifies the perfectly round flowerheads perched on 8-inch (20 cm) stems. Every spring, more

flowers emerge from gradually widening clumps. I love the colors, shades of lilac, lavender and mauve beside a glistening white with a yellow "eye." According to one primula expert, this primrose "carpets the hillsides of the northwestern Himalayas in spring." Must be heavenly.

Although the drumstick primula has recently appeared in catalogs and nurseries, our original batch was raised from seed of the Ronsdorf strain. The word "strain" tells you not to expect uniformity: Some flowers stood out with clearer colors, larger heads, taller stems. These we marked for increase. Division is best done in early June soon after flowering or in late August. Lift the clumps with a small spade. Use a pocketknife and fingers to separate the crowns, making sure that each has as many roots as possible. Replant immediately, and don't skimp on water for the next few weeks.

Like all primulas, denticulatas respond to moist, fertile soil and partial shade. As winter approaches, the long wrinkled leaves die back, leaving next year's buds tightly clenched but visible at ground level. A few mild spring days are enough to coax this impatient perennial out of hibernation and into active growth, making it vulnerable to frost. To ward off the threat, we push 2-foot-long (60 cm) bamboo sticks into the ground among the primulas and drape an old flannel sheet over them on chilly evenings—a bit of work well repaid when the denticulatas are fully out. As one garden writer says, "I know of no more lovely display offered by herbaceous plants for so little trouble as that of P. denticulata."

In front of the drumstick primulas is a sheet of the low and lovely *Primula* 'Mrs. King,' a plant we've enjoyed for many years. The clear mauve flowers, carried singly on short stems, are so thick they hide the foliage. One of the toughest, easiest and most generous spring flowers we grow, 'Mrs. King' is the perfect complement in color and form to the denticulatas behind. Originally from a neighbor, our first clump has been split into the present dozen.

The Japanese star primrose (*Primula sieboldii*) resembles nothing so much as snowflakes—white, mauve and magenta. A bit later than the others, this gradually expanding primula breaks into an exuberant show of fluffy flowers around tulip time—if conditions are right. We thought our original plants were doing well until we moved them out of the sun and into the cool, moist shade under the lilacs; here they are one of the special treats of spring—floriferous, cheerful and care-free. As the primulas fade, nearby hostas expand their parasol of leaves to shade the spot through the hot summer months.

Most of the border-under-the-lilacs holds a collection of seed-raised polyanthus primroses, "polyanthus" meaning many-flowered. An old name, "bunch primroses," describes the cluster of round flowers crowning each stem. Polyanthus come in so many colors (some of them pretty garish) that for the sake of harmony, we edited the list down to cinnamon-brown, reddish brown and honey interspersed with gold-eyed whites as highlights. Naturally, there are plenty of yellows too, and we couldn't resist the blues. (The seeds were Barnhaven primroses "Spice Shades," "Winter Whites" and "Traditional Yellow." For a good selection of seed, consider joining The American Primrose Society, 6730 West Mercerway, Mercer Island, WA 98040, U.S.A.)

Every three or four years, usually in mid-August, when days start to cool and rain is more likely, the polyanthus primroses are dug up, divided and replanted about 8 inches (20 cm) apart in earth revived with organic matter. Deceptively, the little primrose has a weight lifter's appetite. This is the time we play with the palette of colors. To my eye, nothing celebrates spring as beautifully as yellow polyanthus skirting around lavender drumstick primroses.

A PAIR OF BULBS

Two spring bulbs add height and variety of shape under the lilacs. The first is related to the native dogtooth violet, or trout lily (*Erythronium americanum*), a traveling plant that carpets the spring woods with copious copper-and-green mottled leaves but

FACING PAGE: *Related to wild woodland dogtooth violets, erythronium 'Pagoda' opens its sprightly flowers above mottled leaves in spring shade.*

only a few nodding yellow flowers. Among our primroses grows the hybrid *E.* 'Pagoda,' a grander plant with yellow, curled-back petals flecked with cinnamon above wide glossy green leaves. The bulbs have been in place for two seasons and are said to grow easily in rich leafy soil.

More tried and true (also strange and wonderful) is the snakeshead fritillary (*Fritillaria meleagris*), slender enough to rise up through the prim-roses without doing damage. The nodding squarish flowers, dusky plum or white, add a dash of wildness and always draw comment.

LUNGWORTS

Interspersed with the primroses are various lungworts, species of *Pulmonaria*, a valuable but rather ignored group of perennials. Some plants have the weirdest names: liver-wort, bladderwort, spleenwort, lung-wort. "Wort" is an Old English hand-me-down meaning herb, plant or root; you can hear the linguistic connection between "wort" and "root." The references to internal organs come from the medieval Doctrine of Signatures, which theorized that the Creator provided clues to the medicinal use of plants in the appearance of their leaves or flowers. Like a lung, the leaves of many lungworts are cov-

FACING PAGE: *Blue lungwort belongs in shady beds with bloodroot, primroses, trilliums, and such.*

LEFT: *Dainty in appearance yet tough and hardy in reality, London pride expands into a dense ground cover, but it is no match for hostas or vinca.*

ered with tiny filaments and marked with circular gray-white blotches. The name may explain why the plants are overlooked. Unaware of its sterling qualities, your average gardener is apt to walk right past something labeled lungwort on a nursery bench—sounds like something you don't want to catch.

The one lungwort that does get around, especially in older country gardens, is "that spring flower with spotted leaves and pink-and-blue flowers; I've had it for years but still don't know its proper name—my mother always called it Joseph-and-Mary." Or spotted dog or Bethlehem sage or soldiers-and-sailors. This is *Pulmonaria officinalis*, 12 inches (30 cm) high, with heart-shaped dull green leaves heavily splotched with white. For three weeks in spring, a succession of pinkish buds unfurls into small lavender-blue bells —perfectly lovely weaving through the daffodils.

From down home to high-blown Sissinghurst, creation of English gardener Vita Sackville-West: Elegant is the word for *Pulmonaria* 'Sissinghurst White,' with lightly spotted leaves and myriad white flowers. There is something fresh about the green and

white together, a coloring that may be repeated in clumps of poet's narcissus (*Narcissus poeticus*) swaying above. In our Quiet Garden, a wide patch of this lungwort serves as a cover planting for tall white tulips.

Several lungworts go through a pink-to-blue change as they mature, but *Pulmonaria rubra* starts pink and stays that way. Leaves are long, velvety and lighter than most. Always the first to flower, it blooms for a gratifyingly long time. Both 'Redstart' and 'Bowles' Variety' sport slightly darker flowers. The modest bells of rubra might go unnoticed in the rosy confusion of June, but pink is at a premium in spring, when yellow, white and blue predominate. Creamy 'February Silver' narcissus (small, early trumpets), white violets and blue hyacinths make a sweet picture with this lungwort in the shade of a rosy flowering almond (*Prunus triloba*).

If you're partial (as I am) to that deep gentian blue so rarely found in flowers, you'll like *Pulmonaria angustifolia* 'Azurea' even if you can't get your tongue around the name without practice. Leaves are narrow and dark green, and the rich blue blooms spray around prettily on 8-inch (20 cm) stems. Like all lungworts, it is

most effective in a broad swath. For contrast above the pool of blue, I like white 'Thalia' daffodils and, to one side, soft yellow primroses. Try this trio under forsythia. *Pulmonaria* 'Bertram Anderson,' an acquaintance of one season, teams heavily speckled leaves with bright blue blossoms but has not proven too vigorous yet. 'Margery Fish' grows silvery white leaves below nodding pink blooms. Other varieties, all with leaves of varying degrees of green and white and flowers in the pink, mauve and blue range, are worth trying.

As a rule, lungworts are not what you'd call brilliant. Flower tones are somewhat muted; leaves have a matte finish. A single plant makes little impact. But as is often the case, when arrayed in groups of five or more in the dappled light of shrubs or at the front of a shaded border, these useful perennials more than

earn their keep. Their bells ring for three weeks or more, the soft blues and pinks in tune with spring's prevailing yellow-and-white theme. And unlike many spring flowers, lungworts keep up a show of silver-splashed foliage until fall.

Given shade and fairly consistent moisture, lungworts are easy to grow. Soil type is less important than a high humus content: Dig in well-rotted leaves, manure or compost at the start, and spread a layer of the same in fall. Not at all invasive, the plants increase by tiptoeing slowly outward on surface-rooting rhizomes. Division is a simple matter of splitting the rhizomes and setting the pieces a little deeper in a new locale. The work should be done either in June soon after flowering or early enough in September to allow the divisions plenty of time to anchor themselves before winter. Whenever I go to a

nursery, I check the "L" aisle for new lungworts, perennials we now count as indispensable for early color.

LONDON PRIDE

At the edge of our shady spring border grows London pride, commonplace in England but seldom seen here. Why not? This unpretentious ground cover, *Saxifraga umbrosa* in Latin, has lived in the same place for close to 15 years. The patch began as one rosette as big around as a cookie. Pulled apart occasionally as it multiplied, London pride now stretches several feet in all directions. Save for dividing it, I can't recall ever giving this self-reliant perennial any attention at all.

London pride is a true ground cover, spreading laterally to form an unbroken low carpet. The rounded, dark green leaves are serrated along their edges and, in the variegated form that we grow, splashed with yellow. The texture is tough, almost leathery, a quality that keeps London pride presentable year-round. Foliage may be this plant's strong suit, but in late spring, the thinnest of stems rise to 10 inches (25 cm) and twinkle out small white stars speckled with red dots; a burst of stamens at the center of each star gives the spikes a kind of sparkler quality.

Don't count on slow-and-steady London pride to cover great tracts of earth in short order, and don't ask it to compete with hostas or vinca. Instead, give it a shaded home in the company of primulas, dwarf bleeding hearts, bloodroot, trilliums, European ginger, lungworts, and the like. In such a setting, it takes care of itself, keeps its corner evergreen and flowers dependably, asking only benign neglect in return.

DWARF BLEEDING HEARTS

In many gardens, the tall bleeding heart (*Dicentra spectabilis*) plays a notable role in the spring pageant. An exquisite plant it is, with arching stems of gray-green cut leaves hung with finely worked pink hearts. I echo the sentiment of Graham Stuart Thomas, a man who knows his ornamentals, when he says, "A plant in full flower is one of the best sights of spring." If this perennial would hang onto its foliage beyond June, it would rank with peonies for superlative garden value.

Less graceful and showy, but almost more useful from a design standpoint, are dwarf dicentras, which provide a similar charm of foliage and flowers over months rather than weeks. The first we grew was *Dicentra eximia*. Whoever discovered this North American native must have been impressed with it; the surname means "distinguished." In early spring, gray filigree foliage starts to unfurl, and by May, the first

of a long succession of foot-tall (30 cm) stems are dangling their pendants. The color is variously described as pinkish, mauve-pink and light reddish purple, which is to say it doesn't approach the clear rose-pink of dicentra-the-taller. But who can complain when the generous plant often flowers from May to July and beyond? A few years ago, we added the 'Alba' version to a shaded corner of our Quiet Garden; its delicate white blooms (not unlike those of the related woodlander Dutchman's breeches) and gray ferny leaves are company for sweet woodruff and white primulas.

A second North American wildflower, *Dicentra formosa*—its last name means beautiful—has given rise to a handful of named varieties subtly different from each other in

hue of leaf and flower. All are worthwhile, and the choice will probably depend on which are available. 'Luxuriant' is the darkest of all, an unabashed magenta-red. 'Adrian Bloom' sports grayish leaves and deep pink hearts. 'Bountiful' leans to purple, while the leaves of 'Boothman's Variety' are lacy and light gray.

Give these little bleeding hearts the soil and situation recommended for primroses and lungworts if you

FACING PAGE: *A North American native, the shooting star flowers faithfully each April but is slow to increase.*

LEFT: *The rare double bloodroot lasts much longer in bloom than its single counterpart; it may be divided successfully in late summer.*

The Art of Perennial Gardening

can. Cooler, damper parts of the garden suit them best, although they will not complain in a sunny site if the ground is not bone-dry. Our best dwarf dicentra sprang up from seed at the base of a hefty edging rock where it outflowers all the rest; I imagine it enjoys the cool root run and consistent dampness under the rock. Appealing with the smaller bleeding hearts are Spanish bluebells (*Hyacinthoides hispanica*, also known as *Scilla campanulata*), tallest and latest of this family of spring bulbs. Its rose, white and (best of all) blue bells are perfect with dicentra's shades of pink.

PERENNIAL FORGET-ME-NOT

Nothing could be finer spangling through dwarf bleeding hearts than the minute, vivid blue blooms of *Brunnera macrophylla*, a perennial ringer for that small biennial nuisance, forget-me-not (a plant that ensures you never forget it by throwing seed everywhere). Again, the Latin is instructive—*phylla* means leaf and *macro* means big. One old-time writer accuses this plant of "indulging in a summer leafage to which 'Cabbagy' would be flattering" but goes on to say that "this is surely a matter of placing." Placement of choice is moist loam in a shaded border or woodland garden where the large, dark green heart-shaped leaves remain fresh all summer. At Larkwhistle, this fine perennial seeds itself here and there. Although I prefer brunnera as single plants spraying airy bloom among other flowers (like baby's breath in a bouquet), it also works as a long-flowering ground cover if the individual plants are set 8 inches (20 cm) apart. This plant is sometimes listed as *Anchusa myosotidiflora*. Recently, we acquired a variegated cultivar of this name with streaks and bands of creamy white over the green; in a month or so, the costly novelty reverted to plain

green. If *A. m.* 'Variegata' remained bicolored, its splashy leaves would add season-long highlights in a shadowy corner.

BLOODROOT

You could search far and not find a spring flower as compelling as double bloodroot (*Sanguinaria canadensis* 'Flore Pleno'). Actually, you could search far and not find this bloodroot, period. I know it's unfair to rhapsodize over a plant and then say it

may be hard to locate. But think of the challenge, the quest, the thrill of discovery. In the old days, when garden centers were up to their glass roofs in petunias, we looked for some perennials for 10 years or more. The chances of turning up treasures are much better now.

A few years ago, a fellow gardener arrived with a division of double bloodroot wrapped in damp newspaper. Now a sizable clump, this rare wildflower is one of the jewels of May. The single-flowered bloodroot

FACING PAGE: *Odd-looking snakeshead fritillaries are slim enough to come up through primroses in their array of colors.*

LEFT: *Easy to grow, oxlip primroses belong in shady beds with small narcissus and sky-blue grape hyacinths.*

grows in woodlands throughout eastern and central North America. One day, I know not when or where, someone spotted a double "sport"—a naturally occurring variation. All the double bloodroot in gardens today is descended from that single oddball plant. First up are handsome lobed leaves, green hands furled protectively around buds that soon break into many-petaled blooms like small waterlilies. The single bloodroot's delicate, thin-petaled stars with their brush of yellow stamens soon fade;

the double hangs on a week longer.

Garden writer Vita Sackville-West understood bloodroot's gentle appeal: "It is not for people who want a splash of color. It is for people who like looking quietly into the delicacy and subtlety of blue-gray leaves, shell-pink buds and stems whose tender pink seems to complement the opening flowers." She was speaking of the single. Much showier, a colony of double bloodroot makes a solid drift of white, a brilliant contrast with blue lungwort, a subtler match with the pink.

The Art of Perennial Gardening

71

SHOOTING STAR

The sprightly shooting star returns dependably every spring and blossoms quietly in the shade all through May. There is something ethereal about the pendulous flowers, the way the narrow white petals flare back over stamens that come together in a sharp point, like a tiny light-trailing meteor winging through space. Botanically, this is *Dodecatheon meadia* 'Album.' A curious first name: In Greek, *dodeka* is 12 and *thios* means gods; don't ask me who the 12 gods may be or how they came to be associated with this wildflower. "Album" means white; there are also pale pink and purplish forms. The second name is after Richard Mead, an 18th-century English doctor and botanical patron—one of those people who financed plant-finding expeditions and expected some

recognition in return, much like the Renaissance art patron who stares out at you from beside the oxen in a painting of the Nativity.

For us, shooting star neither increases nor dwindles; it just sits tight. Its leaves are long and smooth, gathered into a ground-level rosette. Flower stems rise to 12 inches (30 cm). Although I can picture a woodland floor alight with shooting stars, we are never tempted to divide it. With experience, you learn to "read" a plant, and this one has written all over it: "You get greedy and dig me up, and I'll die on you."

VIOLETS

Spring and violets go together. May woods are sheeted with small yellow and blue violets; isolated clumps of white Canada violets pop through them. In the grass under the

apple trees, waves of sweet violets (*Viola odorata*), both white and lavender-blue, scent the air. We've learned to be selective about which violets we let into flowerbeds. The sweet violet is such a rampant seeder that it was beginning to be a pain in the perennials—better it should live in the lawn.

Violets (as opposed to the annual pansies, violas and Johnny-jump-ups of so many shades and markings) are the kind of flowers gardeners willingly dig up and share with enthusiastic friends. Although we grow a dozen different hardy violets, I would be hard-pressed to give you the names of half of them.

Dipping into a perennial picture book hardly helps—too many lookalikes. Our best is a dime-sized (large, in violet terms) glistening white that soon fattens into showy clumps ripe for splitting. I wish I knew its name. Our nickname, Hanson's White, reminds us of the generous couple who gave us the starter plant. With flowers held well above the dark green heart-shaped leaves, this charmer is ideal for edging a shaded spring border.

Then there is the strange white violet speckled all over with tiny blue spots that looks like a form of the confederate violet (*Viola sororia*) known as 'Freckles'—the name fits, anyway. No such confusion surrounds the Labrador violet (*V. labradorica* 'Purpurea'), a distinctive species no bigger around than a saucer. Purple-tinged dark green leaves would win it space even without its small dark purple flowers. This is not one to plan pictures around but a free spirit fading out in one spot and reappearing elsewhere—always welcome—from seed. A toughie from wildlands as far north as the Arctic, it is still no match for bulky perennials like ferns and hostas. But given a shaded place away from big-leafed floppers, the Labrador violet will no doubt please

FACING PAGE: *Although it thrives in sun, the adaptable pasque flower is an excellent partner for primroses in beds that are not too densely shaded.*

LEFT: *Spanish bluebells—in this case, pink bells—rise through the ferny foliage of dwarf bleeding heart, an easy-care perennial that may flower all summer.*

with its shy demeanor and hearty constitution.

Quite different and thoroughly perennial is the horned violet (*Viola cornuta*), a species originally from mountain meadows—what a picture of wildflowers, rocks and rushing streams those two words conjure up—in the Pyrenees of France and Spain. Running underground, the horned violet sends up small crinkled lettuce-green leaves dense enough for a ground cover. In late spring, a chorus of perky flowers, either white or violet-blue, arises and continues to sing out for many weeks. One writer tells of the plant's "wild floriferousness" in a bed beside an overflowing garden pool. And I remember a particularly wet summer when this violet flowered nonstop for two months at border edge.

More typically, however, our strategy is to cut the plants back by half in midsummer. Then we wait, giving a warm welcome to a second round of bloom when the weather turns cool and damp again.

The Art of Perennial Gardening

Tulip Time

COMPOSITIONS FOR MAY

"Clean and round, heavy and sound, in every bulb a flower."

OLD SAYING

FACING PAGE: *In the company of intermediate irises, early alliums and flowering spring trees, tulips lose much of their stiff formality.*

ABOVE: *Robust foxtail lilies will quickly conceal fading tulips between them.*

ONE FALL ABOUT 15 YEARS AGO, JOHN AND I planted several hundred bulbs among clumps of perennials in two nicely established beds. Spring came. Crocuses and early irises lit up otherwise drab weeks; daffodils added splashes of yellow to drifts of purple and white rockcress and aubrieta. The season was unfolding as planned—a pleasant mingling of colors, a peaceful vista. Until the May morning when a dozen big red tulips opened smack-dab in the middle of the garden. We sat on a bench and surveyed the beds. Tulips were all we saw. Like an alarm bell clanging during a symphony, the unrelenting red grabbed our attention, pushing yesterday's subtle scene into the background. Who would have thought that one group of flowers—maybe it was the center-stage location—could change the whole atmosphere?

"They're so big and healthy," I said,

trying to put the best face on the screamers.

"How about a nice bouquet?" said John, jumping up. In a moment, the tulips were cut. The change was quick and dramatic, as if the garden had breathed a sigh of relief and returned to calm. We certainly did.

Picky, picky, some might say. But no: Making a garden is an exercise in aesthetics, and the process includes your predilection for certain colors and combinations. Until tulip time, color harmony takes care of itself. But enter tulips in all their multicolored finery, and the potential for discord arrives with them. You can't plunk just any tulips anywhere and expect music.

Colors communicate, and they can be at cross-purposes. Red, the most ubiquitous of tulip colors, is the hardest to place. Green is red's most agreeable—certainly its safest—com-

panion, but who wants a green and red garden in merry May? White, lavender and blue also tone down shocking red. Picture red tulips rising through a floor of blue forget-me-nots under the boughs of a white-flowered apple tree (crab or otherwise). If the tulips are crimson (a cool red on the blue side of the spectrum), add a pink bleeding heart. If they are scarlet (a warm red leaning to orange), a white bleeding heart would be better. Red, white and blue may sound a bit too stark and flaglike, but the combination is crisp and flashing.

EARLY TULIPS

Colors, like musical notes, do not have to be close to be harmonious. One of our old gardening books shows a watercolor painting entitled *A Bit of Bizarrerie*: Groups of red and

FACING PAGE: *In light shade, 'Spring Green' tulips create a fresh impression with lacy sweet Cicely and white lamium, perennials vigorous enough to mask the tulips' withering leaves.*

LEFT: *The Lily-flowered 'West Point' is one of the few tulips that harmonize with the acerbic yellow of cushion spurge, a grand perennial that stays neat and green all season.*

white tulips alternate down a border under a wisteria dripping with lavender bloom; patches of purple rockcress and lavender bearded irises are in view. In your mind's eye, replace the white tulips with yellow, and you'll learn something of the difference between contrasting and harmonizing colors. Red, white and lavender complement one another. Red and yellow are in such sharp contrast that no amount of mediating lavender can draw them together. And yet, some people find such a bold opposition of colors altogether stirring. That's the thing about the whole business: *De gustibus non disputandum*—you can't argue with taste.

Here is another red-and-white ensemble, a picture we've enjoyed for many years at Larkwhistle. Every fall, we plant 10 or 12 new bulbs of the crimson early tulip 'Couleur Cardi-nal' directly through a thick mat of double arabis (*Arabis albida* 'Flora Plena') that edges an L-shaped bed. Come May, ruby cups—full-sized from new bulbs, smaller from older ones—float above the fluffy white arabis. Serendipitously, a few sprays of turquoise Virginia bluebells (*Mertensia virginica*)—volunteers from seed sown by birds, breezes or compost—have sprung up. Late white daffodils complete the picture.

The last of the daffodils usually coincides with early tulips, an opportunity for spring scenes of great charm and freshness. The citrus-scented 'General de Wet' tulip, soft orange etched with red, echoes the orange flecks in the double white narcissus 'Cheerfulness,' whose small fragrant flowers are clustered two or three to a stem. Blue grape hyacinths (*Muscari* spp) pool in front; and the brick-red bells of crown imperials

ring in the background, lending an exotic note. A similar match—yellow and blue this time—brings together early yellow 'Bellona' tulips with narcissus 'Yellow Cheerfulness,' grape hyacinths and yellow crown imperials.

The Emperor tulips—red, white, pink and orange—sport large flowers on short stems early enough to companion daffodils. 'Red Emperor' may be the most popular tulip worldwide, but the wide open high-gloss bowls are too much for me. 'Orange Emperor' is another matter altogether, a lovely soft shade that picks up the color of narcissus with orange, apricot or pink cups. Toss in a few turquoise *Mertensia virginica* for an exquisite trio. All Emperors are noted for their tough perennial constitution, a trait that makes them good subjects for planting in the grass of an old orchard with daffodils. In the lawn at Giverny, Monet's old garden outside of Paris, we first saw 'Orange Emperor' growing *sans* label; two years of trying out this and that orange tulip finally landed us with the right one, which now blooms among the daffodils in our orchard.

One of the unsung perennial stalwarts is *Bergenia cordifolia* (once known as *Megasea*), a plant with leathery ping-pong-paddle leaves of a glossy dark green that remain respectable year-round. All through

tulip time, its 18-inch (45 cm) reddish stems carry heads of starry flowers, either white or shades of pink from soft to shocking. Pink bergenia is good company for plum, mauve and lavender 'Triumph' tulips, which bloom just before the tall late tulips. Set bergenia in a group of three or more at the front of a bed to show off its foliage, and be prepared to cut or pull away leaves blotched or blackened by winter. An inch of crumbly compost worked in among the slowly expanding bergenia rhizomes in spring keeps this undemanding big-leafed plant in trim. Tulip bulbs go directly behind the bergenia (or anywhere within view). If the bed veers into the shade, a lovely addition is *Lamium* 'Pink Pewter,' the prettiest dead-nettle around, with silvery leaves and rose-pink flowers. In the sun, double-flowered arabis is a frothy contrast to the more substantial bergenia.

LATE TULIPS

Several dwarf plants and taller perennials are natural companions for late tulips. Perhaps none is as useful as the "moonlit" creeping phlox, *Phlox subulata* 'Emerald Blue,' a silvery lilac that harmonizes with any tulip from strong orange to pale pink. Other suitable foregrounds for matching tulips are white and pink creeping phlox, white candytuft (*Iberis sempervirens*) and strong yellow alyssum (*Alyssum saxatile*). For height, use yellow leopard's bane (*Doronicum caucasicum*), round-headed ornamental onions (*Allium aflatunense*) and pink or white bleeding heart (*Dicentra spectabilis*). Knee-high intermediate bearded irises also flower at tulip time in shades of blue, yellow, purple and pink. Spring-flowering shrubs and blossoming trees lift the eye skyward.

With so many tulip colors to choose from—and so much to bloom with them—the season is rife with pictorial possibilities. Why cling to clichéd arrangements? Decide on a color scheme, gather your plants, and paint away. But be realistic: A couple of planned compositions—three or so different flowers grouped in a frame of vision—will be more satisfying than the busy scattering of disjointed colors, something bound to happen if you succumb to the impulse to try *everything*. Following are some suggestions, both tried and imagined, for tulip-time pictures. The

tulips mentioned are late varieties, tall Darwin, Cottage, Parrot and Lily-flowered types that are the mainstay of May. Naming names is tricky, because varieties come and go, but the current season's selection usually includes more than enough colors to work with.

- Peachy orange tulip 'Dillenburg' next to yellow intermediate irises, with an edging of mahogany viola 'Arkwright Ruby,' on the sunny side of a white-flowered apple or pear tree, either ornamental or fruiting; reaching into the lowest branches of the tree are lavender globes of *Allium aflatunense*.
- Pink and white tulips among three well-spaced clumps of sky-blue *Brunnera macrophylla* (a perennial version of forget-me-nots) next to a pink bleeding heart and backed by *Allium aflatunense* 'Purple Sensation'; along the edge, a stretch of woolly

lamb's ears, *Stachys byzantina* 'Silver Carpet.' Background: lilacs.
- Crimson and/or rose tulips inter-planted with forget-me-nots behind a border of white perennial can-dytuft, with a stand of gray-blue Flo-rentine irises (*Iris florentina*) to one side. Background: pink-flowered crabapple tree or white lilacs.
- Reddish orange tulips such as 'Balle-rina'—a Lily-flowered type with pointed petals—behind *Phlox subu-lata* 'Emerald Blue,' with *Allium aflatunense* in view; dark purple 'Queen of Night' tulips add shadowy complexity where space allows. Background: lilacs.
- Yellow and lavender tulips with a nearby patch of intermediate irises in shades of violet or purple and wands of *Allium aflatunense*, all behind a border of lavender cat-mint (*Nepeta* 'Dropmore Blue'). Background: yellow-flowering

currant (*Ribes odoratum* 'Aureum').
- White Lily-flowered tulips coming through pink lungwort (*Pulmonaria rubra*), with white bleeding heart and Spanish bluebells (*Hyacinthoides hispanica* syn. *Scilla campanulata*) nearby and the unfurling leaves of hostas to one side.
- Mauve and creamy yellow tulips with the white or magenta flowers of silver-dollar (money) plant (*Lunaria biennis*) behind a border of purple rockcress (*Aubrieta deltoidea*). Money plant is a self-sowing bien-nial that can be left to roam within reason—pull out surplus tufts. Background: dwarf early white bridalwreath (*Spiraea thunbergii*)—a shrub to hunt for and treasure.
- White-and-green 'Spring Green' tulips coming through the white-and-green foliage and flowers of *Lamium maculatum* 'Album' in light shade, with creamy lace caps of

sweet Cicely and dainty bells of the summer snowflake (*Leucojum aestivum*) and a foreground of *Pulmonaria* 'Sissinghurst White'—a cool, long-lasting picture that works well in partial shade.

- Light coral tulip 'Rosy Wings' against the green of a hedge (or neutral fence) with a foreground of *Allium karataviense*'s gray-white globes and wide bluish leaves.
- Tall white tulips such as 'Maureen' in front of the pink-wreathed branches of a flowering almond (*Prunus triloba* 'Multiplex'), a sweet shrub seldom taller than 5 feet (1.5 m) that looks like a fountain of small roses in May; a foreground of *Veronica gentianoides* with its myriad slim spikes of ice-blue flowers.
- Groups of dark plum and mauve tulips with a background of the emerging leaves of *Rosa rubrifolia*—a grand shrub rose valued for its dusky foliage—and an edging of rosy *Phlox amoena* and a nearby group of pasque flower (*Pulsatilla vulgaris*), now in its silvery mauve seedhead stage.
- Yellow Lily-flowered tulips coming through the thin-petaled yellow daisies *Doronicum* 'Finesse,' a shorter version of the common leopard's bane, with the blue of mertensia or brunnera spangling through; this bed is planted on the shady side of a garage in a neighbor's garden. Clumps of daylilies could easily take over here in summer.
- Tulips of any bizarre color that takes your fancy with the neutralizing influence of the bulbous *Camassia leichtlinii* 'Blue Danube'—spikes of blue stars on 2-foot (60 cm) stems.

TULIP COVER-UPS

Of all the spring bulbs, tulips are the trickiest to integrate with perennials. It is no coincidence that the geometrical park beds planted solidly with tulip bulbs are promptly dug up once the bloom is off to make room for annuals. Tulips seem made for bedding out on a grand scale. Still, we want them in perennial beds for both their classic cups and their spectrum of colors. Straight-stemmed and somewhat formal-looking, tulips work best in tidy ovals or blocks near the front of a bed. The problem is their tendency to decline after a few years. Granted, this gives us an excuse to try new varieties, but the process of digging up old bulbs and putting in fresh ones can be disruptive to perennials nearby.

What to do? First, there is no harm in doing on a small scale what the parks people do. That is, give tulips their own space, and when they are finished, dig them up and heel them in elsewhere for replanting in fall. Then pop in a few annuals, your own or nursery-bought, to refresh the spot. No harm, but a bother. A better plan may be to plant tulip bulbs a little farther apart than usual—8 inches (20 cm) rather than 5 inches (12 cm)—and then in late May, tuck small plants of annuals such as baby's breath, lavatera, snapdragons, nasturtiums and petunias between them to take over for the summer. Alternatively, you might sow seeds of annuals like cornflowers, nasturtiums, alyssum or cosmos among the tulips. When tulip foliage has shriveled, cut it back to give the annuals more headroom. If tulip bulbs see fit to return next spring, fine.

As a variation, we often overplant tulip bulbs with forget-me-nots, collecting clumps of the self-seeding biennial from around the garden and setting them in place once the tulips are in. The tulips bloom above a sea of light blue, and the forget-me-nots carry on for a few weeks more. Once the forget-me-nots have grown mildewed and seedy, we pull them up—and cut or pull the ripened tulip leaves at the same time—leaving space, again, for a few annuals (bursting their containers by this late date). A similar interplanting tactic can be

FACING PAGE: *Where tulips are planted between perennials such as mounding hardy geraniums and spiky crocosmia, their untidy final act will go unnoticed behind a curtain of fresh green.*

The Art of Perennial Gardening

followed using violas, small annuals that flower for the better part of the summer if consistently watered and deadheaded; choose violas that accord with the tulips' color, and snip away tulip foliage once it has withered, leaving the violas to carry on.

Annuals are one way to go, but some combinations of tulips and perennials work out not badly, as long as you do not count on the picture to last for years and are prepared to renew the tulips as necessary. An example from Larkwhistle: At the edge of a bed of old-fashioned roses are three groups (five plants in each) of the deep-violet perennial salvia (*Salvia* x *superba* 'East Friesland'), a striking foil to the pink roses in June. The spaces between the salvias—blocks of ground roughly $2^1/_2$ feet (75 cm) long by 18 inches (45 cm) deep—are each planted with two dozen tulips. To anticipate the coming pink-

and-purple scheme and harmonize with a nearby bleeding heart, we chose pink, lavender and plum tulips. As the salvias grow, they trail into the tulips' space and conceal their departure; blossom-heavy rose branches also bend forward to close the gap.

Another arrangement of tulips and perennials: In the center of our Quiet Garden is a rectangular concrete pool, a place for waterlilies and goldfish. At one end of the pool, a semicircular bed houses two robust clumps of the spectacular foxtail lily (*Eremurus himalaicus*), a skyrocketing perennial that launches its cylindrical spires of white stars in June. In May, creamy tulips bloom between them, and later, the eremurus's enormous, tuliplike foliage effectively hides the real tulip leaves as they die back. A foreground of white lungwort (*Pulmonaria* 'Sissinghurst White') also fills in. Although we

have them near a pool, both eremurus and tulips originate in hot, dry lands and enjoy warm, well-drained garden soil.

Elsewhere, the elegant foliage—like a silver fern—and the mauve "ragged robin" flowers of the perennial cornflower (*Centaurea dealbata rosea*) make a tallish edging. Behind are clumps of the dependable fall stonecrop (*Sedum spectabile*), gray and respectable all summer, with flat flowerheads maturing from pink to red to rust in fall. Sandwiched in a narrow ellipse between the two perennials are pink tulips set off by silver fore and aft. The cornflower is another of those lax plants that like to recline—a flopper—and here it leans into the tulips with the desired concealing effect.

Many of the perennial/bulb associations suggested for daffodils in an earlier chapter work as well with tulips, except that tulips look like an afterthought when planted in the back sections of a wide border. Pull them forward between front and midsection perennials, or plant them near some octopus-armed thing like Siberian catmint (*Nepeta sibirica*) that will embrace the fading tulips with fresh growth. And be prepared for some delving in the border as the tulip bulbs gradually peter out.

GROWING NOTES

October is tulip-planting time. As a precaution against virus infection, books advise replacing the soil where tulips have previously grown before putting in new bulbs. Being an obedient gardener, I once dug out a wheelbarrow load of "contaminated" dirt and dumped in what I thought would be ideal earth—sifted compost cut with topsoil and bone meal. Into the fluffy mix went a dozen tulips, and I patted myself on the back for being so thorough. In spring, I waited for the happy, well-fed tulips to break through. And waited. Finally, a few sickly leaves emerged and promptly keeled over on rotten stems. The light dawned: I had killed the bulbs with kindness, overfed them, surrounded them with too much rich, damp stuff.

Tulips are native to rocky, sun-baked lands. As such, they need—above all—sharp, swift drainage. To date, our healthiest tulips have grown in ground that was once a gravel driveway—hot, dry and rather stony. In average garden soil, tulips may need very little in the way of extra feeding; a dusting of a balanced natural fertilizer dug in at planting time should be enough. Where soil tends to clay or any degree of damp heaviness, it is a wise precaution to plant the bulbs in pockets of gritty sand. Aiming for 5 inches (12 cm) from bulb top to soil surface, trowel out a deeper-than-needed hole, trowel in some sand, nestle a bulb in the sand, and top with more of the

same before filling in with soil. Protected from decaying damp, the bulbs will send roots into the earth below for sustenance.

In her first book, *My Garden* (1916), Louise Beebe Wilder tells of starting her gardening life "with a prejudice against tulips." Then one spring afternoon, "when taking a walk, I paused to peer over a white picket fence into an old and neglected garden. The tangled area, swept neat by winter's fiercely tidying regime, was presided over by an ancient Apple-tree that seemed, with every twig wreathed in fragrant bloom, to stand lost in an ecstatic dream of its departed youth. Beneath it in the fresh grass, crowding between crimson Peony shoots, were swaying hosts of little scarlet Tulips, 'Brimming the April dusk with fire.'" The scene inspired similar composi-

tions in her garden. The tulip is not without faults, but as another writer notes, "for color that lifts itself up boldly, the heart hungers in May. And then come tulips to satisfy it." Tulips signal that spring's shy, hesitant phase is over. Their multihued display is a kind of overture to summer. And a bit of forethought makes the difference between a whole lot of clash-and-clang and sweeter melodies.

FACING PAGE: *Once the bloom is off, tulips at the front of a rose bed will be overgrown by clumps of perennial salvia and hidden by rose branches heavy with blossoms.*

LEFT: *Tulips—few flowers of the season offer such elegance of form and variety of color.*

The Art of Perennial Gardening

June Tapestry

THE HARMONIOUS HUES OF EARLY SUMMER

"June is so prodigal, so extrava-
gant of all that makes the world
beautiful, so kind to gardeners."

LOUISE BEEBE WILDER

FACING PAGE: *June's bounty includes*
rugosa roses, Siberian irises, catmint,
dianthus, chartreuse Lady's mantle and
fluffy white double dropwort.

ABOVE: *Like a church spire against*
the sky, a white foxglove punctuates
a mass of milky bellflowers.

EARLY SUMMER, AND A BEWILDERING number of perennials vie for a place. Few gardens could hold a fraction of June's largesse. And it doesn't matter. Grow the flowers you most admire in the space you have. Unless you love a wild assortment, it may be more satisfying to bring together a limited number in artistic ways rather than cramming the garden with an over-ambitious jumble. Paring down (and pairing up) the possibilities can be either an occasion for frustration— no one likes to cross off an admirable plant for lack of space—or an exercise in creativity as one mulls over possible combinations. Thinking about each flower in relation to its neighbors—the process of composing pictures—automatically narrows the field. An artistic approach gives you a reason for making choices, whether the goal is to elaborate a color scheme, round out a bed with foliage or introduce more fall flowers—whatever refinements the garden seems to need.

In some ways, a gardening book is like a cookbook. Recipes can be instructive in their own right, even if you never try them. And you probably won't: From any collection, most people settle on a few that appeal and eventually make them their own. In the same way, suggestions for perennial groupings are intended to pique the imagination and give a sense of which ingredients improve each other and generally how they are assembled. Some of the matches described in this chapter we've made in our own garden. Others are fictional, combinations we imagine would work as we observe flowers blooming at the same time but helter-skelter around the garden. That is part of the pleasure of gardening, allowing the imagination to roam, visualizing beds artistically arranged and filled with harmonious color. Sometimes it even happens for real.

There comes a moment in June when the whole garden seems to celebrate the arrival of summer. Poppies pop, irises ripple, painted daisies sway in breezes perfumed by pinks, roses and hardy geraniums begin to bloom, and puffy clouds of meadow rue float over all. It's easy to get all romantic in June, carried away by a month most fittingly described as "bustin' out all over." The spring garden is fresh but not necessarily full. Late summer is usually spilling over but showing signs of seediness and decline. But early summer presents a countenance both fresh and full, an

enthusiastic flowering that can only be met with gratitude.

Louise Beebe Wilder puts it this way in *Colour in My Garden*: "What a chaos of beauty there is upon a June morning! Standing in the midst of the garden, one experiences a sort of breathlessness of soul and sends forth little subconscious pleas to the powers that govern our limitations for more capacity to enjoy the bounty of this glowing, exuberant month." The English garden artist Gertrude Jekyll found her own way of responding to the pageant, wandering around her garden murmuring, "June is here, June is here; thank God for lovely June."

Around the land, a burst of peonies marks the start of summer. Every older garden has a peony or two, nameless old doubles that come up year after year and always end up on the lawn, toppled by a storm so predictable that one of our gardening friends calls it "the peony rain." New gardeners may prefer self-supporting single peonies, varieties that often come with a price tag larger than the roots received. In the long run, any peony is worth growing, both for flowers and for the bush of good leaves, a stable presence in a flower-bed and a screen for more evanescent things behind.

Beyond white, peonies run to pink, crimson, wine-red and magenta. Single or double, the flowers are conspicuous discs of color around which to plan pictures. Although peonies need a lot of sunshine, their blossoms last longer and retain better color if they are shaded for a few hours, preferably at midday or during the afternoon. The same condition suits three of their best companions—meadow rue, hardy geraniums and Siberian irises. Here is a quartet of long-lived, low-maintenance perennials that embellish early summer days and lay a foundation of foliage for the months ahead.

MEADOW RUE

Meadow rues of several kinds are recent additions to Larkwhistle, none as welcome as the so-called columbine meadow rue (*Thalictrum aquilegifolium*), a 4-foot (1.2 m) wildflower from Europe and northern Asia. The surname describes foliage like that of *Aquilegia*, or columbine; at first glance, everyone confuses the two. For lack of a distinct common name, we call this species rosy meadow rue. Spring sees a froth of lovely light

green leaves erupting among daffodils already in bloom. Soon, leafy flower stems, washed with purple as if anticipating the eventual flowers, rise up. By mid-June, a blur of rosy lilac—a softening effect, like mist in the distance—hovers behind full-petaled pink peonies.

Meadow rue's color comes not from petals (which drop unnoticed) but from a mass of stamens. For best color, look for varieties with the

terms *roseum* or *purpureum* appended to their name, or buy plants showing a hint of bloom. Some meadow rues take their cloud resemblance too literally, ending up more gray than pink, but these, too, have a place behind blue Siberian irises. Last summer, we added a white cultivar to our Quiet Garden near a white peony and white hardy geraniums. I can also imagine white meadow rue with pink or crimson peonies, with the lavender bells of tall *Campanula lactiflora*, the milky bellflower, chiming overhead.

A funny story about white meadow rue: One day, my partner came home from a trip to town with the news that he had spotted a white-flowering thalictrum—a single plant—in a tray of mauves at a nursery down the highway. Now, since

FACING PAGE: *Rosy meadow rue lends a light touch to opulent peonies such as 'M. Jules Elie'; meadow rues seldom need staking, while double peonies always do.*

LEFT: *With the June flowering of catmint, painted daisies, single peony 'Mahogany,' Siberian irises and meadow rue, the Rosy Border sings in harmony all along its length; at the edge, pinks are about to pop.*

maintains a show of good foliage through the summer; even its umbrellas of green, then tan, seeds add some color and texture. In our garden, seedlings have sprung up in odd places. So far, we have let them grow, even those blocking the view at the front of a bed. Whether rosy meadow rue will eventually become too much of a good thing remains to be seen. Well described as "dainty yet stately," clumps of meadow rue get better with the years, their mass of foliage more noteworthy, the clouds of color more fulsome. One plant may be enough in a small bed; three, spaced 2 feet (60 cm) apart, have more impact where space allows. Meadow rue responds to decent organic loam, not parched or baked to brick, in either sun or partial shade; staking is seldom necessary.

Says Wilder of thalictrum: "It is the mission ... of certain plants, as it is of certain persons, to make the world ... a pleasanter and more gracious place, not by means of conspicuous achievements ... but by means of more subtle attributes." Meadow rues, she observes, "soften and enhance the landscape, round off the angles, bestow grace and a little sense of mystery where perhaps without them would be brittle contrasts and harsh outlines." So they do.

On a smaller scale in June, the knee-high *Thalictrum* 'Thundercloud' sits neatly at a border's edge or in a cool corner of the rock garden. Its bluish foliage, like a maidenhair fern's, remains fresh into October, long after the puffs of purplish flowers have provided a contrast to the magenta saucers of a dwarf hardy geranium—'Max Frei' or 'John Eisley'—growing beside it. Two other meadow rues (described in the chapter "Midsummer Splendor") bring a degree of elegance to August and early September, a time when the garden may be looking a bit rough and overblown, too yellow and too "daisified."

our garden is more or less full, and since we had more or less resolved to stop collecting every oddball plant that came along—there is, after all, no end to that—he left it on the nursery bench. For days afterward, he wished he hadn't. A week later, I departed for town with instructions to bring home the white meadow rue if it was still there. As I walked into the nursery, I met a gardening friend—herself an inveterate plant collector and, lucky for me, a herb aficionado—walking out of the nursery.

In her hand, she held the white meadow rue. "I just came to get that!" I exclaimed. "You did?" she smiled. "What's it worth to you? I've always wanted a piece of that white-flowered sage you have." It so happened that I had made cuttings from the sage bush a few days earlier. Betting that the cuttings would "take," I agreed to the trade, and my friend cheerfully handed over the coveted meadow rue in exchange for a promise. All the sage cuttings wilted—except one.

After it has bloomed, meadow rue

HARDY GERANIUMS

Some plants grow on you over the seasons. Hardy geraniums may not be flamboyant, but their finely cut leaves, in every case lasting from spring until fall, their long season of bloom and their muted colors have earned them increasingly important roles in Larkwhistle's landscape. Thriving in most soils, in sun or partial shade, geraniums (you'll allow me to drop the "hardy"—we're not talking about summer bedding plants) rarely need watering and are never, in my experience, pestered by insects or disease. Who could possibly ask for more?

Mounding up in front of bushy peonies, straight-leafed Siberian irises or fanning meadow rue and providing a pleasing contrast in form, the dark green hummocks of bloody cranesbill (*Geranium sanguineum*) might be grown for foliage alone. But for weeks, beginning in June, they expand their modest round magenta blossoms. Some folks may find the color crude and hard to work with. Any of the white or purple-shaded Siberian irises harmonize, as does the mauve of meadow rue. Pick your peonies carefully, though, lest their

delicate shades be overpowered by the geranium's harsher hue. The earliest bellflower, *Campanula glomerata* 'Joan Elliot,' tops its lax 18-inch (45 cm) stems with clusters of purple-violet trumpets, a match for magenta geraniums.

While not at all invasive, an established clump of bloody cranesbill can easily sprawl to fill an area broader than a bushel basket. Better behaved—and much more suitable for smaller gardens—are two new compact cultivars, both showing richer colors than the washy tone of the original species. 'Max Frei' grows to all of 6 inches (15 cm) and trails neatly along the ground; a bit taller and bushier, 'John Eisley' reaches 8 inches (20 cm). Set three or more on 18-inch (45 cm) centers in a lightly shaded setting for a fresh effect all season with little work. Beside them might go the sterling ground cover *Lamium* 'Pink Pewter,' its silver heart-shaped leaves a setting for flowers that are rose-pink.

Another treasure among geraniums is *Geranium sanguineum striatum*, once known as *G.s. lancastriense*— sorry, I cannot find a common name. Pale pink saucer-shaped flowers delicately etched with crimson lines

FACING PAGE: *In light shade, the elegant bluish leaves and purple puffs of thalictrum 'Thundercloud,' a dwarf meadow rue, companion geranium 'Johnson's Blue.'*

LEFT: *Where white flowers predominate, more attention is drawn to flower form and subtle variations in shading. In our Quiet Garden, foliage plants such as hostas and grasses are as necessary to the overall impression as the peonies, hardy geraniums and other perennials that bloom in June.*

The Art of Perennial Gardening

shine against dark green foliage. At a height of 12 inches (30 cm), it is shorter than its parent but billows out to fill a 2-foot (60 cm) circle. Seldom without a smattering of bloom, this fine perennial belongs in the front row, where its lacy leaves might contrast with the substantial foliage of hostas, dwarf daylilies and bergenia. A crisp effect comes from growing this light-colored geranium in front of a dark red peony. Siberian

irises of any hue would harmonize in this setting, and I would want a meadow rue in the picture too. Afternoon shade is best, but otherwise, this geranium, like its kin, wants only good soil and neglect. Once it has settled in, it hates above all to be moved, an act sure to sever the plant's long taproot and sorely set it back.

No color caveats come with the white form of the bloody cranesbill

(*Geranium sanguineum* 'Album'), a perennial that highlights any planting. In our Quiet Garden, a drift of white geraniums, over a decade old and still in good shape, spills over the edge of a raised bed with a well-staked white peony behind. In the same frame of view are white Siberian irises, a white rugosa rose and a clump of Japanese silver grass (*Miscanthus sinensis*). The same white geranium makes a fresh picture with a pink peony and blue Siberian irises, with rosy meadow rue behind.

Beyond the *sanguineum* group are other geraniums, grand and small, for sun or partial shade. Big fluttery flowers—pure white cups beautifully veined with lilac—belong to *Geranium clarkei* 'Kashmir White,' a newcomer to our garden. In one season, it joined the ranks of favorite perennials. Leaves are deeply cut and dense enough for ground cover. Reaching to knee height, this vigorous plant creeps about on rhizomatous roots in a manner that may spell trouble in smaller gardens. Last summer, cooler and damper than most, 'Kashmir White' flowered continuously from late May until well into July; six weeks of bloom, generous in the world of perennials, is more typical. If you enjoy (as I do) the bold contrast of deep, rich colors highlighted with white, juxtapose this geranium with a dark violet bearded iris such as 'Dusky Dancer'—see that the geranium does not overshadow the iris roots—and a crimson peony. If foliage is a first priority, substitute a Siberian for the bearded iris. One geranium, one peony and three iris roots will get you started.

The tallest geranium we grow, and the most oddly colored, is the Armenian cranesbill (*Geranium psilostemon*). Standing waist-high, the bush of sharply incised leaves, each as big as an open hand, is topped with clusters of round flowers of a shocking dark magenta-pink made more dramatic by contrasting black centers—a hard one to companion. I don't see pairing this geranium with orange lilies, as one writer suggests. Next to crimson peonies, it looks muddy. At Larkwhistle, the strange color is matched with blue Siberian irises and pale yellow early lilies; I can imagine it, too, with rosy meadow rue and white Siberians. To keep it from leaning on its neighbors, the tall plant needs the support of three slim bamboo canes wound around with string at several levels. Like many geraniums, its foliage takes on red tints in fall.

At the other end of the ruler are two dwarf geraniums, ideal for small beds or a rock garden that is not too sun-baked. For years, we have enjoyed *Geranium cinereum* 'Ballerina' growing with other miniature perennials in a rock-paved space in front of a garden bench; an enclosing arbor provides some shade. Bred at Bressingham Gardens in England, this 6-inch (15 cm) geranium displays small maroon-veined pink saucers centered with darker color, a flower that invites close scrutiny; its gray-green leaves are round and frilly. Similar but with darker flowers and less conspicuous veining is 'Lawrence Flatman.' Both want perfect drainage—gravel and grit are better than clogging clay or manure—and hate winter wet. Companied with these geraniums under the arbor are flat mats of mauve creeping thyme, purple-leafed Labrador violets, the silver rosettes and dainty white flowers of lime-encrusted saxifrages and a small version of London pride. Here, as well, are two exquisite dwarf pincushion flowers, *Scabiosa columbaria* 'Blue Butterfly' and 'Pink Mist,' both about 1 foot (30 cm) tall; if deadheaded faithfully, these dainty perennials keep sending up more round, flat flowers stuck all over with tiny pale yellow stamens like pins. In a small bed, the bluish leaves and wispy purple of 'Thundercloud' thalictrum, mentioned above, might form the background of this scaled-down picture.

SIBERIAN IRISES

Over years of tending and observing a garden, you gradually learn who (as they say) your real friends are—plants that return faithfully each year, keep their foliage for the better part of the season and do not speedily overgrow their allotted space, menacing neighbors and forc-

ing you to dig them up for division or eviction, plants that want only reasonable care in exchange for flowers and bring a measure of grace and elegance to the garden without burdening the gardener. When you find yourself repeatedly splitting a particular perennial (even though you don't have to) and spreading it around the garden, you know you've found an ally. The Siberian iris is tailor-made for beautifying gardens large and small, whatever the soil and no matter what the winter is like. They grow best in moist, fertile, humus-rich soil in sun or light shade, spaced 2 feet (60 cm) apart at the start.

For foliage effects, both simple and enduring, Siberian irises excel, their sheaves of reedy 3-foot (1 m) leaves lasting well into autumn. Flowers come in June, lightly fashioned irises in shades of blue, mauve, purple,

wine and violet, as well as white. Specialty catalogs list dozens of cultivars. Of the ones we grow, let me put in a good word for 'Orville Fay,' medium blue and flaring; 'White Swirl,' wide white petals with a yellow blaze on the falls; 'Super Ego,' a large dramatic dark blue; 'Fourfold White,' broad-petaled, almost flat flowers from a vigorous plant; and 'Big Blue' (what more can I say?).

COLOR SCHEME
FOR EARLY SUMMER

June may be the month to aim for that impressionistic ensemble of pinks and blues, crimson, white, cream and lavender—romantic hues that belong to early summer. A pink or crimson peony might be the centerpiece. Behind it, set one to three plants of rosy meadow rue; in front of the peony, arrange a spread of white

geraniums or the light pink *striatum*. Flank the peony to one side with one or more Siberian irises—blue, white or violet. Bulbs of various kinds can be tucked in for spring (see the chapter "Fade Out, Fade In"). A few later perennials—daylilies, a clump of aconite and some coneflowers—will complete an easy-care assembly that gives a long season of interest in relatively little space.

Such a scene can be spun into a more elaborate tapestry by drawing in other matching flowers of the season. In the background, shrubs add stability and height, none better for our present purpose than *Rosa rubrifolia*, a tall but contained bush that seldom outgrows the confines of even a small garden. Its small matte-finished leaves show a subtle overlay of colors—washes of purple, blue and gray—like the skin of a plum. The strong-growing rugosa rose 'Jens

Munk,' laden with round double pink flowers in June, would do as well; this is my favorite of the double rugosas, my only complaint being that the old flowers hang on untidily, whereas singles such as 'Scabrosa' and 'Frau Dagmar Hastrup' drop their petals cleanly. For ease of cultivation, it is often wise to leave a walking (at least a squeezing) space between background shrubs and perennials in front.

Taller than meadow rue by a head and an ideal companion in color and form, the milky bellflower (*Campanula lactiflora*) consorts beautifully in the back row, nodding its branching cones of clustered lavender-blue bells over peonies and Siberian irises in front. This long-lived perennial—"One of the finest," says Graham Stuart Thomas—always draws admiring attention at Larkwhistle; many visitors mistake it for a shrub when the panicles of flared bells are at their height. Left unstaked (as it often is in our garden, not for lack of willingness but for lack of time), some branches are sure to bend toward the ground; the effect is either a graceful cascade of color or a tangle, depending on whether we get breezes and showers or winds and driving rain. A couple of tall bamboo stakes and

some twine make all the difference. Otherwise, this bellflower is carefree and permanent in good loam and sun or light shade. "A magnificent plant for associating with shrub roses, it thrives anywhere" (Thomas again). And, I would add, a perennial to search for, place carefully and then leave in peace: "They should be left without division as long as they are doing well," according to one expert. There are several named varieties that show stronger colors or slightly larger flowers.

Every bit as tall and just as enduring, the giant goat's beard (*Aruncus dioicus*) forms a handsome leafy clump as big across as your outstretched arms; this is a perennial that needs room to expand. Come June, its great creamy plumes wave in the wind like an enormous astilbe for 10 days or so, fading gradually to rust. When the plumes turn frankly brown and messy—and we get past pretending they are adding anything resembling "textural interest"—we snip the flower stems off, leaving the mass of good foliage, almost shrublike in substance, to decorate an angle of the Quiet Garden until November. I read that goat's beard is "inclined to sulk in hot summer areas

The Art of Perennial Gardening

unless planted at the waterside or in peaty, moist soils." Our single plant—and one is plenty unless you are landscaping an estate—does well in ordinary loam without undue attention or extra watering. Another expert concurs: "[It] thrives in any soil, moist or dry, in sun or shade." Cream-colored goat's beard looks splendid mingling with the lavender of the milky bellflower. It might also grow behind another of June's bellflowers, *Campanula latifolia*, a first-rate clumping perennial that dangles large tubular bells of deep purple-violet along the top third of its 4-foot (1.2 m) stems. This plant has a white form that gleams in a clearing of a neighbor's woodland garden—and, mysteriously, in our Quiet Garden too, where I swear we never planted it. In a bed outside the Quiet Garden grows the purple *latifolia*; seeds must have fallen through the lattice fence, and

oddly, the resulting plants bloomed white, as if "aware" of the theme in that enclosure. Don't ask me—I just work here.

Keeping with our rosy color scheme but moving from the back of the bed to the middle and front areas, we have a number of medium-height perennials to consider. The deep burgundy leaves of *Penstemon digitalis* 'Husker Red,' a choice 30-inch (75 cm) newcomer from the University of Nebraska, stand out in front of the green of Siberian irises; pale pinkish white tubular blooms are arranged in slender spikes. At least three plants set 1 foot (30 cm) apart are needed for an effective show. In a sunny garden, the seldom seen *Lychnis flos-jovis* 'Hort's Variety' adds woolly gray leaves and round, dark rose flowers in clusters on 2-foot (60 cm) stems, an excellent edger for dry ground. We grow this lychnis directly in front of

a single-flowered 'Mahogany' peony, its crimson petals so translucent that they glow like a circle of ruby around straw-yellow stamens when the sun shines through.

More mauve can be found in the ragged-robin blooms of the 30-inch (75 cm) perennial cornflower *Centaurea dealbata rosea*, free-flowering and easy, with leaves like a silver-green fern. One or two plants may be enough; a few twiggy branches keep their flower stems from sprawling (but we never get around to this job of staking either). A more compact cornflower is *Centaurea* 'John Coutts,' named by Graham Stuart Thomas after the late Curator of Kew Gardens in London. Excellent for massing either in the middle of a bed or at the front, its fluffy deep mauve flowers are centered with white above foliage more green than gray. Both these cornflowers should be deadheaded

FACING PAGE: *Both rosy meadow rue and chartreuse Lady's mantle work well in a variety of June scenes, especially those containing roses.*

LEFT: *Peonies and roses typify the hues of June; a tall Prestonian lilac peeks over the fence.*

regularly and tidied up after they finish flowering—trace the flower stems down into the foliage, and snip them off along with any yellowing leaves. Other than that, they look after themselves in the sun.

Rose and crimson are the colors of painted daisies (*Chrysanthemum coccineum*), a reliable and very showy midborder perennial. I've noticed that the plants do much better with clear space around them than if lost in a jumble fighting for sun. Some light support—bamboo and twine or twiggy brush—keeps them upright. A welcome foil in color and texture comes from mounding catmint (*Nepeta* 'Dropmore Blue' or other named varieties); their dusty pebbled leaves and haze of tiny lavender flowers may not dazzle, but they do soften and enhance whatever grows nearby. This is not something we would fuss over, but nepeta is so easy in any

sunny, drained site that we welcome its modest appearance year after year, spilling over the edge of various beds and harmonizing with all.

The same might be said of Lady's mantle (*Alchemilla mollis*), except that its froth of flowers is a light greenish yellow—just the shade to take some of the sweetness off all this pink— spilling over handsomely pleated leaves at the front of a bed. So roundly reliable, so neutral in color it fits anywhere, Lady's mantle comes to mind as a possible candidate whenever I'm looking for a relatively short easy-care perennial for important—or problem—spots around the garden. The temptation is to overdo it, to lean too often on this dependable plant instead of scouring around for something else. At least that is the gist I get from the other gardener every time I suggest Lady's mantle in a new place—"Not *that* again. Can't you come up with something new?"

Which reminds me of a principle of design for those tending extensive gardens: It is seldom a good idea to repeat the same plants over and over in different parts of a large garden. As one old book quaintly puts it, "Let not everywhere each beauty be espied." Whether in color or kind of plants featured, distinct sections should be just that—distinct. There will then be a sense that an area was developed for a particular reason: to play with a color scheme, to showcase a collection of roses or alpines or simply to make room for new plants.

Back to June. Double dropwort and *Filipendula hexapetala* (and *F. vulgaris*) 'Flore Pleno' are the odd names, common and Latin, for a tough perennial like Lady's mantle in height and lightness of floral effect. This time, though, foliage is deep green and finely divided, like a dense bunch of carrot tops; tiny round pinkish buds open into sprays of fluffy ivory-white bloom. ("What are those flowers that look like cottage cheese?" one visitor asked.) Pretty in a mass—three to five plants spaced 12 inches (30 cm) apart at the edge of a bed—this Asian native (which I've also seen under the name meadowsweet) teams up well as an edging plant with our core quartet of the season: peonies, Siberian irises, meadow rue and geraniums.

Lavender and silver seem natural companions for pink, whether literally lavender bushes with their gray foliage and roses or the same shades in other flowers. Some plants impress on first sight. Last fall, I dug three bulbs of a new 3-foot (1 m) flowering onion, *Allium* 'Beau Regard' into the middle of a 4-foot-wide (1.2 m) island bed. This June, three balls of lavender bloom, round as small cantaloupes, hovered above the lacy leaves of *Artemisia* 'Lambrook Silver' growing to one side. Packed with hundreds of the small star flowers typical of alliums, 'Beau Regard' kept its color for

weeks; seedheads left until they fell apart looked like static tan-gold sparklers. At $12 a bulb—the price we put on rare things—these were no cheap onions, but if the bulbs multiply as we hope, they will have been well worth it. Although these bulky bulbs need some space—1 foot (30 cm) between them is about right—no harm is done if a light foliage plant such as 'Lambrook Silver' artemisia (best of the aromatic family) leans over them. The ground-level allium leaves are of no account and soon disappear altogether. A similar allium, the slightly taller 'Globemaster,' flowers more mauve than lavender; its bulbs dropped dramatically in price after two years as supply increased. Not rare at all and impossible to kill, common chives contributes small round heads of light mauve in early summer. For deeper rose flowers, look for the new 12-inch (30 cm) cultivar 'Forescate,' just as tasty as ordinary chives but much showier.

Of the 15 or more alliums growing at Larkwhistle, none shines like our old friend *Allium christophii* (which used to be *albopilosum*, "white and fuzzy"), an onion that has decorated the front of a bed of old roses for almost 20 years without attention. Each June, the big spherical heads— loose clusters of light lilac stars glinting with a metallic finish—find a way through the tangle of rose canes, violet spikes of *Salvia* 'East Friesland' and the octopus branches of blue Siberian catmint. Some years, there are more alliums, some years fewer.

Older bulbs may die out while new ones grow from seed and through the process of underground expansion. We leave them alone. While not as obviously stunning as 'Beau Regard,' *christophii*, a native plant in Turkey, retains the charm of wildness. Alliums love fertile ground, not too heavy or wet, in the sun, or to quote from an old source, "The Onion requireth a fat ground well digged and dunged." Well digged and dunged might be the key to successful gardening in general.

This is not the sum of early-summer bounty available to gardeners who love pink, blue, purple, violet, lavender, and such. Space allows only a brief recapitulation of other candidates discussed in greater detail in our first flower book, *The Harrow-*

smith Perennial Garden. From tall to short, June brings to the garden:

- *Eremurus himalaicus*, foxtail lily or desert candle—5 feet (1.5 m): Skyrocketing spires thickly set with star-shaped white flowers. Plant fleshy roots in fall in very well-drained soil in the sun. Lovely behind pink peonies with meadow rue or the milky bellflower or both.
- *Anchusa azurea* syn. *A. italica*, Italian bugloss—3 to 4 feet (1 to 1.2 m): Small brilliant blue six-petaled flowers massed over branching and somewhat floppy stems. A coarse but showy short-lived plant that comes back in unexpected places from seed.
- *Valeriana officinalis*, garden heliotrope or valerian—3 to 5 feet (1 to 1.5 m): Wide, flat heads of pinkish white, like oversized Queen Anne's lace, add lightness to a planting of peonies or Oriental poppies. Roving roots and seeds may pose a problem, but unwanted plants are easily turfed out. Most people enjoy the pervasive scent of this old-fashioned flower, so there must be something wrong with my nose—I find the fragrance heavy but inoffensive on the breeze and smelly as a cat's litter box close-up.
- *Iris* spp, bearded irises—3 to 4 feet (1 to 1.2 m): Bred in every color of the rainbow. Pick the shades you like for whatever scheme you are planning—a nice way to choose irises is to visit collections at their height of bloom in botanical gardens or specialist nurseries.
- *Papaver orientale*, Oriental poppies— 3 feet (1 m): Salmon-pink cultivars of this well-known perennial team up with 'Lambrook Silver' artemisia, woolly lamb's ears or other gray-leafed plants. Says E. A. Bowles: "The pink of the Oriental Poppy in the midst of all this silver foliage looks simply delicious, like a strawberry ice on a frosted glass plate." Deep crimson poppies are almost shocking in contrast with

FACING PAGE: *The oddly shaped pinkish blooms of gas plant (center) harmonize with painted daisies, pinks and blue Siberian irises. Gas plant should be situated carefully and left to develop in peace.*

LEFT: *Blooming almost a month after rosy meadow rue, airy Thalictrum delavayi sets off the hot pink of lobelia 'Rose Beacon.'*

foreground of Lady's mantle and a backdrop of old roses.

- *Aquilegia alpina* 'Hensol Harebell,' blue columbine—3 feet (1 m): A tough, healthy columbine that comes up wherever it likes from seed, dangling deep lavender blooms with fine effect among the rosy throngs of June. This long-lived variety seems immune to the insects that often chew fancier long-spurred hybrids.
- *Salvia* x *superba* syn. *S. nemorosa*, perennial salvia—30 inches (75 cm): Adding shadowy depth to a rosy scheme, 'East Friesland' is one of the best cultivars, with its massed spikes of small deep violet flowers set in purple bracts. A fair bit taller, the marginally hardy 'Miss Indigo' glows richly next to pink or dark red peonies, contrasting completely in color and shape.
- *Geranium himalayense* 'Johnson's Blue'—2 feet (60 cm): A popular geranium for its long season of blue saucer-shaped flowers. At Larkwhistle, this vigorous perennial has grown for years adjacent to a pink peony with rosy meadow rue behind. Left unsupported, its stems sometimes topple over—the casual look. The plant should be tidied up once it starts to look unsightly.
- *Heuchera* spp, coral bells—18 inches (45 cm): Tiny pink or red bells are light as sparks in front of heavier blooms; I find them useful for hiding the bare lower stems of peach-leaved bellflowers. A host of new heucheras, conspicuous for decorative leaves—waved and ruffled, shades of green or variously colored and zoned—has recently appeared. 'Palace Purple,' named for Kew Palace, where its seeds were first collected, has proven popular for its burgundy foliage and tiny white blooms; it needs massing in fertile soil in sun or light shade. The similar 'Palace Passion' has pinky red flowers over wine leaves, while the related *Heucherella* 'Bridget Bloom'

white Siberian irises and the violet spikes of *Baptisia australis* or perennial salvia. Set poppy roots close behind clumps of the showy fall stonecrop (*Sedum spectabile*), which will grow up to hide the gap left by the disappearing poppies.

- *Dictamnus fraxinella* (*D. albus*) 'Ruber' or 'Purpureus,' gas plant—3 feet (1 m): A very long-lived perennial with fine foliage all summer and spikes of interesting reddish mauve flowers lined with deeper color in June. Position gas plant

carefully in rich ground in the sun, and do not casually move it around. Well-companioned with rugosa roses, the cream-and-white striped foliage and informal lavender flowers of *Iris pallida* 'Zebra,' hardy geraniums and painted daisies.

- *Campanula persicifolia*, peach-leaved bellflower—3 feet (1 m): Lavender-blue or white wide-open bells face out from thin, self-supporting stems. Gradually expanding clumps are pretty in light shade with foxgloves or in sun wedged between a

waves wands of light pink above marbled green leaves for many weeks. All should go at the front of a bed to show off their foliage.

• *Gypsophila repens* 'Rosea,' pink creeping baby's breath—12 inches (30 cm): At the edge of our Iris Border, this low, early baby's breath drapes a shoulder of limestone with a shawl of thin leaves spangled all over with small pink blooms; light and airy, it sets off the stiff sword leaves and full flowers of dark violet bearded irises growing behind. A delightful perennial for sunny, well-drained places, it also comes in white.

• *Dianthus* spp, pinks—8 inches (20 cm): For the same sites as baby's breath, the gray grassy mats are studded with simple, sweet-scented round flowers in white or shades of pink through June and into July. Shear back after flowering for compact growth and better wintering. I cannot imagine the early-summer garden without waves of dianthus lapping along border edges, wafting their clove fragrance into the air.

MIDSUMMER SPLENDOR

COMPOSITIONS FOR JULY AND AUGUST

*"By August, a flower garden…
can be at its best—and at
its worst. Most of one's
successes are apparent,
and all of one's failures."*

KATHARINE S. WHITE

FACING PAGE: *Pink bergamot and white
Asiatic lilies are ideal companions;
feverfew in front adds a light touch,
although its seedlings may become
a minor nuisance.*

ABOVE: *A portrait of the colors of midsummer: Dark pink yarrow, blue
veronica and white daisies.*

IN THE GARDEN, CHANGE IS CONSTANT. FOR a time, we regret the fading of daffodils, the way lilacs and peonies turn from petals of glory to crumpled brown. But change sparks our interest; there is always something to look forward to. Walking through our garden at the end of June, noticing all the perennials about to bloom, a friend commented: "There's such a sense of promise now—so much hope." As June bows out, the many intriguing buds of midsummer begin to color and expand.

There is nothing too subtle about the colors of July and August. Gone are the tender shades of spring and the sweet rosiness of early summer. In their place are rich, saturated colors— violet aconites and delphiniums, the hot hues of daylilies, the unabashed magenta and salmon of phlox, red bergamot, all those yellow daisies. The making of a riot is at hand. But

so is the potential for the special resonance of strong colors in combination—a harmony of contrasts.

STARTING WITH DELPHINIUMS

Perennial pictures presided over by delphiniums are bound to be lovely— the tall spires thickly set with sky-blue, navy, violet or lilac florets are without peer. Staking, though, is a must—two or (better) three tall canes per plant encircled with soft string at no fewer than three levels. The task is less fumbly if the delphiniums are accessible, not stuck away (as they are here) at the back of a bed up against a fence (which is, of course, the logical place for them). Conventional wisdom says that delphiniums are short-lived, but such information usually seeps up from the south. In cooler areas—that is, much of Canada, New England, the prairies and the West

Coast—delphiniums should be as perennial as anything else. With us, they usually come back for five years before heading into a crowded decline. At that point, we divide and renew our favorite colors; occasionally, we'll buy new plants in spring for fresh stock.

The verticality of delphiniums is accentuated by flowers with other outlines, none as effective as yarrows, daylilies and lilies. Yarrows combine beautiful shades with strong horizontal lines. Lily and daylily flowers are open and flaring in form, and a daylily plant gives an overall impression of roundness. There are a number of ways to juggle these four elements.

Of all delphinium colors, I am fondest of the light blues and the dusky violets. In front of violet delphiniums, white regal lilies (*Lilium regale*), their long perfumed trumpets washed outside with light purple and

FACING PAGE: *July brings daylilies, phlox, dark monkshood and red bergamot to a corner of the garden that has already been through several stages of flowering.*

LEFT: *There are few perennials that display the sumptuous colors and stately form of delphiniums.*

centered with yellow, contrast sharply in both color and form. Flank the lilies with yarrow—pinkish lilac, cerise-red or the buff-yellow 'Great Expectations.' Along the front, the succulent wine leaves and reddish purple stars of *Sedum* 'Dragon's Blood' pick up the purple on the lilies' outer petals. Like all sedums, it gives no trouble as long as it can see the sun and keep its toes fairly dry. A very different impression results when dark violet delphiniums are fronted by light yellow lilies with an edging of chartreuse Lady's mantle.

For a softer picture—a classic combination of blue, white and pink— start with light blue delphiniums, and face them down (once again) with regal lilies or another white. To one side goes 'Salmon Beauty' yarrow, its flowers fading from light salmon to pinkish buff like a shirt that has gone through the wash many times.

The flowerless lamb's ears (*Stachys* 'Silver Carpet') shine at the edge. If this quartet blooms within sight of a 'New Dawn' climbing rose, its glossy green canes dripping with pale pink roses, you have created enough beauty for one season. As an alternative to yarrow, use pink bergamot (*Monarda* 'Marshal's Delight'), one of the most useful and decorative perennials of midsummer. Be prepared to curb the spread of both yarrow and bergamot every other spring.

If you do not have room for delphiniums or lack the patience to stake them, bring in some veronicas, sun-loving perennials of easy culture in any well-drained site. Flowering in shades of blue, they send up thin spikes useful for contrasting with yarrow, lilies and daylilies. At roughly 3 feet (1 m), *Veronica longifolia* is one of the tallest; hybrids such as 'Sunny Border Blue,' 'Goodness

The Art of Perennial Gardening

Grows' and 'Romiley Purple' show deeper color than the species. With an edging of 'Dragon's Blood' sedum, any of these might spire in front of regal lilies. The blues of veronica also complement Asiatic lilies, whether yellow, orange, amber, pink or dark red. With these two, I like the white discs of double Shasta daisies.

The arching leaves and funnel flowers of daylilies in all their fruit-bowl shades—cherry, melon, apricot, orange, lemon, banana and peach—call for the vertical lines and neutral tones of veronica. In one of four perennial beds in the middle of our Kitchen Garden, the useful apricot daylily 'Stella d'Oro' is matched with 'Salmon Beauty' yarrow and burgundy outfacing lilies. *Veronica* 'Goodness Grows' adds spikes of blue, while white Shastas are in view across the path. There is something so simple and summery about such combinations, the kind of old-fashioned scenes that have delighted flower lovers for generations.

WHITE MULLEIN

Mulleins are aspiring plants *par excellence*. In a family of tall yellow biennials, the white mullein (*Verbascum chaixii* 'Album') is an oddity. At 3 feet (1 m), it is the shortest. Better yet from a gardener's point of view, it comes back every year. From a rosette of broad ground-hugging leaves grow self-supporting tapers strung with white blooms centered with purple stamens. I love to see the white candles rising into the light lavender bells of tall *Campanula lactiflora* (see previous chapter). In front of the mullein, set a clump of early daylilies, any of the peach or melon sorts, full-sized or miniature. Augment their warmth with a few clumps of scarlet Maltese cross, its glowing umbrellas held a little above the daylilies. White, lavender, peach and scarlet—for me, these are the colors of July.

A most useful plant for midsummer compositions, the white mullein forms a backdrop for golden knapweed, a tall cornflower with whimsical yellow puffs perched on round bracts, brown and dry as old parchment. Here, too, are strong-growing rust-red daylilies, yellow Turk's-cap lilies and a froth of Lady's mantle in front. Even two or three of these elements will make a pleasing picture. Given a fair degree of sun and ordinary soil, white mullein will last for years and spring up on its own from seed. It may, in fact, become another of those pretty nuisances which every gardener copes with, plants like Johnny-jump-ups that you want around for easy color but that cause no end of friendly feuding.

MONKSHOOD AND COMPANIONS

Every summer, I am impressed again by the beauty and usefulness of monkshood. Aconite and wolfsbane are other common names for the genus known botanically as *Aconitum.* At present, six different monkshoods decorate our garden. Cousins of delphiniums, they are tall plants adorned with scores of flowers ascending wiry stems. Upright as a church steeple, the leading shoot gives rise to shorter side steeples,

keeping the plants in bloom for a surprisingly long time. Fashioned like an intricate puzzle, the individual flowers merit a close look. Two small winglike petals hang down from the base of two larger petals that arch together to form a flattened, open-ended tube. The curled-back lips at the front of the tube form an entrance for bees to crawl through for nectar. Shielding the tube is an overhanging hood shaped like a monk's cowl or a knight's metal helmet.

For best display, set aconites in fertile, moisture-retentive soil; a summer mulch and a weekly soaking during dry spells also help. Although aconites will grow in sun, they seem happier in partial shade; in deep shade, says one writer, "the evil beauty" of the darker kinds is accentuated. This sinister reputation is related to a lethal poison found in the turniplike roots.

The first monkshood we grew (and one that is still a favorite after 15 years) goes by the name *Aconitum*

napellus 'Bicolor.' A lovely 5-foot (1.5 m) perennial—and potential background for many midsummer pictures—it gives rise to spires of navy-and-white flowers above dark green, deeply fingered foliage. Just as sump-

FACING PAGE: *Blue-spiked veronica complements the warm tones of daylilies; 'Paprika' yarrow heats up the composition, while self-sown alyssum and California poppies fill in the gaps.*

LEFT: *Airy baby's breath always adds a touch of lightness when grown with more substantial flowers such as lilies.*

tuous in its dusky cloak is a pure violet monkshood, which (after years of
anonymity) seems to match the
description of *Aconitum henryi*
'Spark's Variety.' If pressed to choose,
I would pick these two over others
for their long flowering and wonderful color.

Here are some suggestions for
using monkshood to advantage with
other perennials. In each case, the
aconite goes at the back; companion
flowers are noted in order of descend-
ing size. Blue-and-white aconite
sparkles behind red bergamot—
either 'Cambridge Scarlet' or the
mildew-resistant 'Gardenview Scarlet'—with a foreground of white
Shasta daisies. To tone down the picture, replace red bergamot with pink.
Lovers of pink might like to see dark
violet aconite behind the big trumpets of 'Pink Perfection' lilies with
pink bergamot to one side and a wave

of pink baby's breath (*Gypsophila*
'Rosy Veil') in front; because of the
lilies and baby's breath, this picture
needs a fair bit of sun.

For years, we have enjoyed a corner bed shaded by an old crabapple
tree where both violet and blue-and-
white monkshoods lean over clumps
of white phlox. In front of the phlox
are three daylilies—yellow, peach
and light orange. To one side is a
stand of red bergamot. Melon-colored
daylilies feathered with red are luscious in combination with dark
aconite and white phlox or with
aconite alone if you've given up
phlox on account of mildew. Indeed,
any planting of daylilies, whether
massed or small-scale, would be
improved by aconites waving above.

The salmon-orange of tiger lilies
(*Lilium tigrinum* or *L. lancifolium*), a
color difficult to companion, looks its
best mingling with blue-and-white

aconite. As one old-time writer noted,
"The more the two spread and crowd
each other, the more splendid is the
display." This old-fashioned lily is
damned in some quarters as a "vegetable Typhoid Mary," a carrier of
viruses that could infect other lilies.
When garden health is an issue, late-
blooming Asiatic lilies in all their
warm reds, yellows and oranges
could easily substitute for tigers as
companions for monkshood.

At the back of one of Larkwhistle's
narrow borders stands a tall midsummer perennial—with great jagged
leaves and wide fluffy panicles of
pink, like cones of candyfloss or an
ostrich-feather boa—that always
draws admiration and comments
from visitors. This is Martha Wash-
ington's plume, better known as
queen of the prairie (*Filipendula rubra*
'Venusta'). A spectacular native plant
for moist, even boggy sites, the queen

FACING PAGE: *Heavy-headed phlox needs lighter flowers such as baby's breath for company; steel-blue sea hollies and late meadow rues also counterbalance the phlox's solid shape and strong color.*

LEFT: *White flowers such as echinacea and Oriental lilies have a cooling influence in the dog days of August.*

might consort with violet monkshood and look down from her great height over pink bergamot, pink and white coneflowers (*Echinacea*) and any of the cherry or magenta (but not salmon) phloxes. Closely planted corms of dark purple or lavender gladiolus—I like a miniature called 'Blue Jeans'—grow as vertical ribbons through this richly woven tapestry.

PHLOX SEASON

Gardeners aiming for color rapport in an area that can be seen as a whole from any vantage point— whether an entire backyard or a single bed in a larger garden—have choices to make for midsummer. I'm not alone in observing that the most jarring color combinations result when pink and magenta tangle with yellow and orange. In older gardens, magenta phlox and orange tiger lilies are the standard-bearers for the two camps. Both sides are well represented in July and August, with the edge going to the yellow-and-orange team—all those rudbeckias, sunflowers, daylilies, lilies, yarrows, and such. A color-sensitive gardener—though admittedly, there are many who couldn't give a fig for this kind of

"quibbling"—may have to pick sides, whether rosy or sunny, cool or hot. Since the cooler shades of midsummer are less familiar, let me lead you down that path and suggest some compositions that revolve around phlox, that great exemplar of midsummer pink.

To complicate matters, the various phloxes bicker incessantly among themselves, some leaning toward orange and scarlet, others dipping into purple, mauve and pink. At present, our garden holds five different shades of phlox besides white: a sizzling pink on the salmon side, an equally hot coral-pink, a piercing deep magenta, a pretty light rose and a washy lilac. Magenta and salmon glare at each other across a path like feuding sisters; coral burns up her corner, while rose and lilac, by comparison, fade into the background. All our phloxes came from friends' gardens; none have real names (the phloxes, not the friends). Every summer, for the sake of harmony, I'm tempted to remove all but my favorites, magenta and rose; but I have yet to meet a gardener who can, in good conscience, rip out perfectly healthy perennials just to satisfy a color sense. It seems we remain gar-

The Art of Perennial Gardening

deners first and picture-makers second, even when phloxes turn their rouged cheeks away from our best efforts at matchmaking.

Selecting phlox in bloom may be your best bet. Once you have found a shade or three you like (and that like each other), the next step is to get them hitched with sympathetic partners. In partial shade, aconites are ideal with phlox; the monkshoods' upright lines relieve the phloxes' wheel-like regularity—round flowers in rounded heads. Blue-spiked veronica does the same in the foreground. I am exceedingly fond of a tall native plant that we first met as *Veronica virginica*, or Culver's root; its new first name is *Veronicastrum*. Given reasonably good ground, damp rather than dry, it grows into one of the unassuming beauties of summer. Narrow, pointed, dark green leaves are arranged in whorls all the way up wiry stems, which continue to stretch into long, thin spires set with tiny silver-white flowers. Gold-tipped stamens poke out of each bloom, giving the inflorescence a light, bristly look. Completely winter-hardy, Culver's root grows into large clumps that can be left alone for years. Nothing is finer beside or behind phlox in a lightly shaded situation; violet aconite could easily make a third.

FACING PAGE: *A nameless old red daylily forms part of a warm assembly with fluffy yellow knapweed and lemon downfacing lilies.*

LEFT: *The odd salmon-orange of tiger lilies meets its match when crowded among the blue-and-white monkshoods; both do well in rich ground in lightly shaded places.*

Out in the sun, the jagged, spiny gray leaves and round steel-blue flowerheads of globe thistles (*Echinops ritro*) are a dramatic counterpoint in shape and color for phlox; the two are matched in height. The neutral influence of grasses, either tall miscanthus behind or blue oatgrass (*Helictotrichon sempervirens*) in front, allows strong-colored phloxes to shine unchallenged. In the middle of our Old Garden, magenta phlox gets along nicely with neighboring sea lyme grass, whose silver blades trail in the phlox's dark green foliage. In the same picture are two annuals that hold their own among the more settled residents. Few annuals are as showy as lavatera 'Silver Cup.' From July until hard frost, it unfurls bright pink funnels like small hibiscus flowers veined with maroon; a lighter zone leads the eye to the flower's center, where a cone of pink stamens grows from a wine star. Cosmos, too, weave thread-leafed branches through our phlox and float mauve or wine-red flowers among them. Both annuals are easy as anything from spring-sown seed.

Perhaps my favorite companion for phlox is sea holly, not the big alpine type, but any of the small-flowered sorts, *Eryngium amethystinum, E. planum, E. tripartitum* or their hybrids. Little thistly heads, each perched on a prickly metallic blue ruff, decorate multibranched blue stems. Compared with the round solidity of phlox, sea hollies appear airy and sort of comic. Literally stiff and dry, they come across as light and delicate. All sea hollies appreciate a fairly sunny, well-drained place in ordinary ground; division is neither necessary nor desirable, and the plants do not care to be moved around.

For years, we have enjoyed the August display put on by so-called dwarf delphiniums. Named varieties of *Delphinium grandiflorum*, whether 'Blue Butterfly,' 'Blue Elf' or 'Blue Mirror,' are among the jewels of midsummer. Standing thigh-high, they are dwarf only in comparison with their lanky relatives. Above finely cut greenery, the plants break into a crisscrossing network of wiry branches, closely hung with open-faced blooms tinted the vivid deep blue of spring gentians—a rare color at this time of year. Although reliably perennial, younger plants put on the best show. At Larkwhistle, new plants pop up from seed, and the occasional sky-

The Art of Perennial Gardening

blue sort appears among the dark blues. Both are beautiful next to rose phlox, with crowns of pink bergamot in sight. In a hot, yellow month, we turn gratefully to this trio of cool pinks and clear blues, more so when their bed is shaded from the afternoon sun by nearby lilacs.

GROWING PHLOX

I don't understand phlox. In at least three farm gardens around here, they grow lush and strong in long hedgelike rows. As far as I can tell, they are never fussed over and probably not divided on anything like a regular basis. Every August, the green rows become wide ribbons of crimson, magenta and lilac. At home, in flowerbeds, phloxes seem to exhaust the soil—maybe it's our sand—and themselves after a few years; clumps grow overcrowded, lower leaves turn yellow, the odd stem wilts, and mildew may creep in with the humidity. Still, they are worth the effort, for no midsummer perennial is quite as spectacular. Without phlox, August would lose much of its vibrancy and cheer.

I have a feeling that phlox prefer the splendid isolation of a bed apart; certainly they need their own space in a mixed border. First, give them room, about 2 feet (60 cm) all around per plant; sun or light shade is fine. Next, they are hungry: See that the soil is well supplied with organic matter at the start—a big bag of store-bought manure should feed three. A handful of fertilizer scratched around each clump in spring and a 1-inch (2.5 cm) top mulch of compost, old leaves or manure can only help. Plants should be divided (say the experts) every three or four years, very early in spring; lift the old clump, slice off a lively looking segment, and return a chunk with three to five shoots.

A tip: If you do not get around to dividing phloxes, and the shoots are coming up thick and weak, thin them when they are about 6 inches (15 cm) tall; reach in and pinch out, as close to ground level as possible, half or more of the shoots, the weakest ones and many from the plant's center. This goes some way toward preventing mildew. Other preventive measures include planting phlox where air circulates well and soaking the ground around them faithfully at least once a week during dry weather—do not sprinkle from above or spray around with the hose in the evening, leaving wet foliage open to fungus all night. Some phlox varieties are much more mildew-resistant than others, and it is worth seeking them out. Ask friends and neighbors—with luck, one of them will say, "Mildew on phlox? What's that?" Ask at garden centers, too, about natural fungicides such as sulfur or baking soda. For the most part, our phlox remain mildew-free until September, when a few warm, drizzly days may promote a crop of fuzz on the leaves. But by then, we're not all that concerned.

MIDSUMMER MEADOW RUES

There remain two more excellent companions for phlox. Rosy meadow rue belongs to June with peonies, Siberian irises, and such, but other thalictrums infuse the August garden with a similar elegance. First comes the 5-foot (1.5 m) *Thalictrum delavayi* (sometimes known as *T. dipterocarpum*), discovered in western China in 1890 by a certain Abbé Delavay. Like all meadow rues, it exhibits a special charm of leaf, like a maidenhair fern with a slight bluish cast. Waving above the foliage is an open, interlaced web of branches spangled all over with exquisite small blooms, five-petaled stars of clear lilac, each with a central tuft of pale yellow stamens, the whole creating what one writer aptly describes as "a great airy-fairy pyramidal display." All the flowers hang down, so you look up to see the stars emitting their tiny beams of light. A week later, double-flowered meadow rue (*T. delavayi* 'Hewitt's Double') comes into bloom. Multiplied 20-fold, the lilac petals are turned from stars into small balls of color, gossamer as baby's breath but tall and pale purple—an altogether lovely creation.

When associating meadow rue with phlox, situate the phlox to one side so that meadow rue's foliage is

FACING PAGE: *A cool August effect is assured when 'Blue Butterfly' dwarf delphiniums and pink bergamot share a bed; rosy phlox will soon join them.*

LEFT: *With magenta phlox, purple gladiolus, blue sea holly and annual cosmos, airy 'Hewitt's Double' meadow rue brings refined color to a season that is often dominated by yellow.*

evident. And be sure to pick your phlox color with care. Thalictrums stand out next to soft pink or white phlox, and dark magenta throws the lighter meadow rue into fine relief; but next to shocking salmon and coral phloxes, gentle meadow rue appears pale and retiring.

In the rough, untidy month of August, these two thalictrums lend an air of freshness and poise. But their finery is not to be had for slap-dash planting in any old dirt. Meadow rues grow best in deep, rich earth fattened with old manure, thoroughly rotted leaves, and the like; lime is to their liking. One expert recommends enriching an area as you might for a clematis (see following chapter), planting thalictrum in a hollow about 8 inches (20 cm) deep and filling in with good soil as it grows. A summer mulch keeps the soil cool and moist, and a twice-weekly soaking promotes steady growth. Good drainage, though, is a must; in heavy, clogged ground, meadow rues are apt to rot over win-

ter. At Larkwhistle, 'Hewitt's Double' puts on a splendid show in a sunny bed in company with magenta phlox, sea holly and lavender gladiolus. Its single-flowered counterpart grows in light shade. As woodlanders, meadow rues may prefer a cool, lightly shaded site—not dankly overhung with hungry trees but the kind of flickering shade cast by shrubs and trees at a slight distance. If sun is your lot, choose an open, breezy place, not the grueling hot spot on the south side of the house. Where strong winds blow, the tall stems may need some support. Our clumps lean on each other and into the arms of a young cherry tree beside them, but we also poke a few bamboo canes into the ground among them, weaving the canes through the tangle of stems.

All meadow rues should be sited carefully and then left in peace. They improve with age.

COOLING TOUCHES OF WHITE

The hot colors of midsummer need all the cooling a perceptive gardener can provide. White flowers help. Mention has been made of the cool silver-white of Culver's root (*Veronicastrum virginicum*) as a foil for hot pink phloxes. In light shade, Culver's root works equally well in the back row neighboring blue-and-white aconite, with red bergamot and

peachy daylilies in front. Another spiring plant for summer shade is black snakeroot (*Cimicifuga race-mosa*), a native wildflower in eastern North America. Its tall ivory spikes, like skinny bottle brushes, rise with fine effect behind the broad leaves of hostas. Mercifully, it needs no staking. Snakeroot's divided dark green leaves form an attractive clump the season through. Woodlander that it is, the plant adapts to dryish ground but grows wonderfully lush where its roots can search out moisture.

Very much at home in a damp, semishaded position, the graceful gooseneck flower (*Lysimachia clethroides*) begins to open the first of a long succession of white star flowers in August and continues into fall; because the *passé* blooms drop off cleanly, the inflorescence—in profile like the head and beak of a goose— always looks as if it is just coming into flower. Gooseneck flower spreads quickly from the root but is not hard to dig out. Once more, hostas might furnish the foreground. A few clumps of the well-nigh indestructible spiderwort (*Tradescantia* spp) add grassy foliage and small triangles of blue and white to this shady-side picture.

In the sun, tall milky mugwort (*Artemisia lactiflora*) waves its creamy plumes of tiny blooms above most other flowers. Coloring in August and September, this species is a lovely backdrop for the round flowers of helenium in their array of reds, rust, orange and yellow. A few weeks earlier, the first-rate artemisia hybrid 'Guizho' cools the warm colors of daylilies, red bergamot, crocosmias, heliopsis and rudbeckias. Shorter than the species, 'Guizho' is sure to become a familiar presence in gardens as it becomes better known.

Gossamer baby's breath (*Gypsophila paniculata*) and its varieties blur edges and tone down stronger color wherever they grow. Sun and deep, gritty soil supplied with lime are needed to bring the grand airy clouds to full potential; leave gypsophila alone once it puts down roots. Compositions that include the cooling touch of gypsophila are as varied as the perennials of midsummer. For sentimental reasons, let me mention one: I always enjoy the romantic look of tall sky-blue delphiniums and deep red lilies near an arbor draped with pink rambling roses; hovering lightly among them is a gray-white cloud of baby's breath.

The Art of Perennial Gardening

HOT AND DRY

DROUGHTPROOF PERENNIALS FOR SUMMER DISPLAY

"The threat of shower activity has passed, and it looks like a gorgeous weekend."

WEATHER FORECASTER

FACING PAGE: *Woolly mulleins, low thymes, sedums and yellow yarrow all do well in dry, gravelly ground.*

ABOVE: *With careful choices, there need be no shortage of color in hot, dry locations.*

PLANTS ARE CLEVER CREATURES. OVER MIL-
lennia, they have adapted to life in
every variation of soil, light and climate, save for those rare landscapes
that are continually snowbound and
frozen solid. Lucky for gardeners. We
need only delve into books, nurseries
and friends' gardens to find some
flower that is bound to flourish in
whatever combination of earth and
exposure—whether perfect or piti-
ful—that we're attempting to beautify. To a large extent, site will deter-
mine the character of a garden; it
will, that is, if you are clever enough
to work with what is given.

Our garden lies fully exposed to
the sun. Over the years, annual help-
ings of compost, rotted leaves and
manure have improved the soil, but
still we are working with a sandy
loam that tends to dryness. A rainless
week or two in midsummer sets our
worry engines whirring. Short of an
elaborate system of hoses and sprin-
klers, there is no way we could water
the entire garden. And even if we
could, we'd be reluctant to tax the old
farm well to that great an extent. All
our neighbors say it's a fine well—
full of water, never gone dry—but
we'd rather not test the limits. Does
this sound familiar? In many places,
the wise use of water is an issue, and
rightly so.

Happy the gardener who learns
early to sidestep frustration and futile
effort by concentrating on plants
suited to the conditions at hand. Special treatment is fine for a pet perennial or two, but a big garden full of
delicate wilters and fussy eaters soon
becomes a burden. With our open
site and light soil, we needed a core of
camel-like perennials that could go a
long way in the sun and sand on little
water. And a curious thing has happened: Perhaps out of sheer gratitude
for their self-sufficient ways, we have
come to regard many of the droughtproof perennials as favorites. As I
haul water from garden pool to
flowerbeds in an attempt to keep the

thirstier aconites and heleniums in
trim, I give the lavender, pinks,
yarrows, baby's breath, herbs and
sedums an appreciative glance—and
a miss, as if to say, "Look at you, flowering away. I don't know how you do
it—that soil must be dust—but carry
on." And they do.

Plants know a trick or two about
water conservation. In a nutshell:
Catch what you can, and store what
you've got. Gray foliage is a case in
point. Gardeners gravitate to silver
leaves for the cool sheen they bring.

But gray foliage is a plant's evolution-
ary response to particular conditions—hot and dry. The gray coloring
is due to the presence of countless
tiny hairs on a leaf's surface; many
gray leaves are noticeably downy to
the touch ("pubescent," as a botanist
would say). The hairs trap airborne
moisture and reduce transpiration of
water from the leaf. And while dark
green absorbs heat, silver tends to
reflect, which keeps the leaf a little
cooler. There is no shortage of silver
to decorate dry, sunny gardens. For

shimmering effects, look to the following groups, each of which has a number of members: achillea, arabis, artemisia, catmint, cerastium, dianthus, grasses, mullein, rue, sage and stachys.

As they adapted to dry lands, some plants evolved small, tough leaves less dependent on water for their growth. Many Mediterranean cooking herbs—thyme, savory and oregano, to name three—as well as lavender and baby's breath fit this model. In contrast, sedums and sempervivums (hens-and-chicks) store water in leaves that are succulent to the touch and juicy when crushed. Roots, too, act as water reservoirs: The rhizomes of bearded irises and the bulky tuberous roots of daylilies, desert candles, spurge and peonies all hold moisture against inevitable dry days, as do bulbs of lilies, daffodils, ornamental onions, and the rest.

Often it is a good strategy to group plants of a similar character together—small alpines among rocks, moisture lovers in a deep bed of retentive loam (perhaps by a pool), droughtproof perennials in a bed that you need never water. Some gardeners are so hooked on hoses that the thought of not watering may strike

them as strange: Surely such a bed would look tired and brittle, dry as a desert, if rain failed for a few weeks in July. True, no perennial will live indefinitely in a completely parched environment—even camels have limits. But eventually, rain clouds gather, and the garden is refreshed. Until that happens, certain flowers are able to see to their survival without so much as a drop. Two Larkwhistle borders illustrate the point. Both our Iris Border and Yellow Border come through the driest summers without supplementary water (which is different from saying they aren't better off for regular rainfall). When other parts of the garden appear to be suffering from heat and drought, these areas remain fresh and presentable.

THE IRIS BORDER

As you come into our garden from the road, you pass along a narrow west-facing border that catches the sun from dawn till dusk. Under a thin layer of sandy topsoil lies a foot of gravel, remnants of an old driveway that once led up to the farmhouse. Drainage is not a problem here. To demarcate the border from the lawn,

ers over juicy reddish green globules; and prettiest of all, *S. kamtschaticum* 'Variegatum,' with succulent green-and-gold foliage and yellow flowers that turn to star-shaped red seedpods. Because sedums are so easy to propagate—*too* easy, you'll be thinking as round leaves break off, roll away and root where they land—gardeners are forever handing along anonymous shoots to curious (but unsuspecting) friends. One of our best sedums is officially nameless (but looks a lot like *S. aizoon* 'Aurantiacum'). Its succulent blue-gray leaves are a year-round feature, and every July, yellow flowers open from reddish buds. The blue stonecrop (*S. reflexum*) is here too: small, bluish, rice-shaped leaves all year and yellow blossoms in summer. Even our native sedum, the bitter stonecrop (*S. acre*), forms a small pool at the edge, its round, gray leaves hidden once a year by lemon-yellow bloom. Both thymes and sedums love to hug warm rocks and spill over the miniature cliff faces with fine effect. Together they create an easy-care border edge of great character and interest. Occasionally, some thymes need to be replaced after a bad winter; the sedums are more likely to need containing.

Sprouting through and just behind the thymes and sedums is a conga line of early snow crocuses—white, cream, lavender and purple; the wee bulbs present no threat to the stronger perennials that expand to hide their dying leaves. If space allowed, we would shift two excellent plum-and-rose sedums from other parts of the garden to round out the collection: *Sedum* 'Ruby Glow' grows round leaves shaded like the skin of a red plum; its dusky pink flowers appear in August and September, when dwarf pink perennials are rare. Darker yet and earlier-flowering is *S.* 'Vera Jameson.' Both die back to tight tufts every winter and regrow vigorously in spring; both show deeper coloring in hot,

we laid down a line of chunky limestone rocks and raised the soil 8 inches (20 cm) above grade. A raised bed is warmer and drier yet.

That long rocky edge seemed perfect for thymes, small Mediterraneans partial to hot sun and light, gritty ground. In went groups of silver-leafed thyme, lemon thyme, caraway thyme—three of the best for seasoning. In went nonculinary creeping thymes—green, golden and woolly-gray, bushy or flat as a rug. Over the summer, the thymes twinkle out flowers of lavender, white, mauve and deep purple. A single genus, *Thymus*, offers a variety of leaf and flower colors, textures and scents. (For a full discussion of thymes, please refer to *The Harrowsmith Illustrated Book of Herbs*.)

For a change, we alternated thymes with low-growing sedums, another group of dry-weather friends. Here you find *Sedum spurium* 'Dragon's Blood,' with maroon foliage and wine-red star flowers; the fast-spreading *S. album*, with white flow-

dry spots. Some gardeners scorn sedums as being undramatic and offering little challenge, but I'm all for modest perennials that make no demands—especially under such difficult conditions.

At regular intervals along the edge of the Iris Border are dark green mounds of creeping savory (*Satureja reptans*). Oblivious to scorching sun and dry weather, this aromatic herb begins to open dainty white flowers in late August and continues beyond Thanksgiving. Green all season, flowering late, unfazed by drought, perfectly perennial and useful in cooking—what more could you ask of a plant? In spring, we vigorously tousle the winter-dried stems, snapping them off and clearing them away to make room for fresh growth. If I had a hot, dry (and weed-free) slope to cover—perhaps the side of a raised septic bed in sun—I would work up a stock of creeping savory and the stronger creeping thymes, plant them on 8-inch (20 cm) centers and tuck masses of snow crocuses between them.

Prominent at intervals behind the edgers are symmetrical hummocks of cushion spurge (*Euphorbia polychroma*), a knee-high perennial that is

so old-fashioned, it is due for a comeback. Simple light green leaves dress strong stems from the ground up. In late May, lacy greenish yellow flower caps perch atop the stems. In truth, these are not flowers but *bracts*, showy pseudoleaves that sit just below the inconspicuous real blooms. Coming early, cushion spurge is a natural companion for tulips. But choose your tulip shades carefully, since most clash badly with the spurge's unusual yellow. Our best tulip picks so far are the clear yellow 'West Point' and the safe 'White Triumphator,' both Lily-flowered types with pointed petals; these are set in large groups behind the euphorbias. I'm open to suggestions, but any other tulip colors would probably be a fright with the acid-yellow.

In front of each spurge are colonies of early peachy red *kaufmanniana* tulips and blue glory-of-the-snow, easy spring bulbs that bridge the gap between the April crocuses and the tulips of late May. After the spring flower show, cushion spurge rounds out like a leafy footstool, obscuring the maturing tulips in front and behind. By the first of June, there have been three waves of color—nothing splashy or intricate,

but something to enjoy. The spurge stays neat, green and self-contained (and unwatered) until its leaves turn yellow in fall—it is a most valuable perennial.

At one time, this border grew only bearded irises in all their rainbow hues. The name remains, but over the years, we have thinned the iris clumps to make room for later perennials. Still, I can't agree with the writer who maintains that the bearded iris looks "like a flower designed by a cow." Some are surely overblown and strangely colored, but the tri-part form, embellished by breeders with graceful ruffles and curves, remains one of nature's extraordinary beauties. I love the colors too: clear yellows, pure blues and deep violets, the mahogany-reds, the coffee-and-golds and the one with cloud-white standards and sea-blue falls. Unharmed by drought, bearded irises are tailor-made for a dry, sunny spot. A fierce hardiness and fairly decent summer foliage also keep them in perennial favor.

With the irises blooms a lilac-colored yarrow, a variant of *Achillea millefolium*, the native white yarrow of fields and roadsides. In sandy soil, its roots run quickly and may need curbing every few years. Friends and neighbors will soon be telling you thanks but no thanks as you try to pawn off surplus yarrow. A compost heap is no place for the well-nigh indestructible roots. Put what you don't need in a cardboard box by the roadside, and eventually, yarrow will beautify the town dump. Our lilac yarrow was chosen as the best color from a batch of "Summer Pastels" raised—they practically raised themselves—from seed. Unless you're prepared to be ruthless and toss out many interesting but unspectacular seedlings, I do not recommend the yarrows-from-seed route.

"You know, I like yarrow well enough," a visitor told me, "but I finally dug mine out; it takes up too much space in a small garden." A big garden like ours can stand a traveler or two, and I would want a patch of yarrow in a smaller place, too, for the pretty shades and its long-flowering habit. Just keep an eye on it. Recent hybrids of *Achillea millefolium*—creamy 'Great Expectations,' scarlet-red 'Paprika' and (my favorite) pinky buff 'Salmon Beauty'—are a little less "spreadacious" but every bit as drought-tolerant.

Lilac yarrow flowers into July, contrasting in shape and color with fragrant regal lilies (*Lilium regale*) planted beside them. Although lily bulbs hold a supply of moisture, the big flowers are sensitive to dry weather. If drought descends while the lilies are in bud, they may drop a few buds and concentrate their energy on the rest—four or five blooms per stem instead of eight or ten. Lily bulbs like sharp drainage and warm soil; in damp, heavy ground, they are prone to rot.

Wedged up against the split-rail fence that backs the Iris Border, tall mulleins (*Verbascum* spp) raise aloft branched candelabras lit with yellow flowers in July and August. A welcome vertical element, the mulleins have reseeded for years. Every year, we avail ourselves of a handful of small plants and move them into vacant spots for next year's flower-

ing. You learn to be less sentimental after a while: Unnecessary mullein seedlings are weeded out by the score. Branching Greek mullein (*V. olympicum*) and woolly white Turkish mullein (*V. bombyciferum*), the two we started with, swap pollen freely, and plants with characteristics of both routinely appear. All mulleins are happier in dry, hot soil; anything remotely clogged or sodden may do them damage. Most are biennial—leaves one year, flowers the next, end of plant—but two splendid perennials are described below.

The Iris Border is only 3 feet (1 m) wide but runs a length of 60 feet (18 m). For effect and emphasis, the pattern of plants is repeated three times down the border—three groups each of lilies, yarrow, cushion spurge and attendant tulips, with irises between and odds and sods of mulleins filling gaps. The same sequence of bloom could be accomplished in a border one-third the length. A few years ago, we shifted a variegated Japanese silver grass (*Miscanthus sinensis* 'Variegatus') to one end as a kind of finishing touch, a definite stop. Living here, it will have to adopt the camel ways of its companions.

THE YELLOW BORDER

Where two keen gardeners work on one place, there is always a lively—who said *heated*?—exchange of ideas, a sharing of enthusiasm, a compromise of tastes. But sometimes, it's fun to have a space of one's own, a canvas where you get to express some quirky aesthetic without consultation or debate—who said *fight*? To one side of the vegetable garden, John has made a Rosy Border, turned out in shades of pink, mauve, crimson, violet and blue. In a new border on the opposite side, I get to be the boss and make all the decisions—and do the work. The site is typically sunny and, lacking the benefit of years of organic enrichment, is drier

FACING PAGE: Yarrows, such as the lilac variant growing here with regal lilies, may be too invasive for small gardens, but few perennials take to dry sites as successfully.

than other parts of the garden. Partial to yellow and lavender flowers combined with silver foliage—and knowing there would be many candidates for a warm, dry bed—I settled on a color scheme. To simplify maintenance, there would be no bulbs (a decision I hated to make because I want spring flowers everywhere). At 10 feet (3 m) wide and 40 feet (12 m) long, the border is big. The plan was not to water.

At one end of the border, against a cedar-rail fence, is a back-row group of 'Harison's Yellow' rose. One of the old "farm" roses, it develops into a fair-sized shrub and sends out suckers to boot. Rooted stems from an older overgrown bush provided a fresh start for this winter-hardy rose. Blooming all at once in June, it erupts with such fluffy yellow verve that its arching branches turn into flower-wreathed garlands. 'Harison's Yellow'

makes the best of any soil; we've grown it for two decades and never once watered it.

FRONT ROW

The front line of the Yellow Border consists of four stalwart, drought-tolerant perennials. 'Moonshine' yarrow I have always admired for its feathery sterling-silver leaves and flat heads of lemon bloom. Three plants set 18

inches (45 cm) apart soon grow into a close-knit, weed-suppressing unit. When flowerheads fade to brown, I trim those stems away, leaving the foliage to shine on into fall. So useful and easy is this yarrow that the groups are repeated three times along the edge. Also repeated, but as single plants, is *Nepeta* 'Blue Beauty' (sometimes listed as 'Souvenir d'André Chaudron'), best of the ornamental catmints. Its stems are clothed with gray pebbly leaves that are as aromatic as you might guess from the name; each stem ends in a spire of small lavender flowers that open over many weeks. One plant expands to bushel-basket size. In color and form, yarrow and catmint do nice things for each other. Some gardeners, though, may not appreciate the air of wildness about them, their lack of refinement. Both tend to sprawl, so they are better beside an earth, brick or gravel path; the designated mower will not appreciate their lounging on the lawn. Early spring is the best time to plant or divide these two.

Down the line, where the border turns a corner, is a spread of plush lamb's ears, the flowerless 'Silver Carpet.' I like the flowering version too, both for the small mauve blooms always abuzz with bees and the vertical lines it brings to the front of a bed next to round lavender bushes (another candidate for hot-and-dry). But gardeners who appreciate lamb's ears' long silver leaves more than its flopping flower stalks should look for 'Silver Carpet.' After a hard, damp winter, be prepared to restitch the best-looking scraps of the carpet into a more seamless whole. Any healthy-looking remnants—even a few leaves with roots attached—can be lifted and shifted and will soon weave themselves together into a ground-hugging rug. About the only thing that will kill lamb's ears is too much water, whether winter damp or summer flood. There is—horrors—a yellow-leafed lamb's ears that you might think would be a natural in a yellow border, but to my eyes, it looks like a dead thing. Why anyone would want to turn a perfectly good gray-leafed plant yellow, I can't say.

MIDDLE ROW

In the middle section of the Yellow Border, several clumps of yellow loosestrife (*Lysimachia punctata*) light up in June, the starry flowers on 3-foot (1 m) spires fine companions for 'Harison's

Yellow' roses behind. This loosestrife is a coarse, strong plant that prefers damper ground—it "has become a ditch-weed" in parts of England, says writer Graham Stuart Thomas—but gets by on minimal water. Better for "wilder parts of larger gardens," it fills in anywhere, needing only division every four or five years and the support of a few twiggy branches pushed in around it. Hardiness guaranteed, but think twice if you tend a smaller garden.

An undisputed treasure, though, is a fantastic flowering onion imperiously named *Allium* 'Globemaster.' I'm always a bit suspicious of a new variety that arrives on the scene surrounded by a lot of hoopla and adjectives. Only a writing assignment could have forced me to shell out $25 for one bulb. But when that bulb hoisted a fat 3-foot (1 m) stem carrying a cantaloupe-sized ball of lilac stars the following July, we had no choice but to be duly impressed. When one bulb turned into four by the next year, we thought "good investment" and promptly spread them around. What a visual feast this early allium makes wedged between 'Moonshine' yarrow in front and yellow loosestrife and yellow roses behind—one of those easy flowery pictures you remember fondly in winter and look forward to seeing again. All alliums are at home in light soil and sunny places. Dormant for half the year, they store a supply of moisture to draw on during drought.

In three places through the middle of the Yellow Border are plants that you might guess were daylilies from the look of their long, strap-shaped leaves. These are torch lilies, also known as redhot pokers. Once called *Tritoma*, the genus has been renamed *Kniphofia*. The cultivar is *Kniphofia* 'Primrose Beauty,' an acquaintance of four years. Every August, 10 or 12 thigh-high stems emerge, each topped by a bottle-brush cluster of

pendulous, tube-shaped, light yellow flowers. Every winter, we cross our fingers. The northern limit for the various kinds is listed as zone 6 or 7, only occasionally zone 5. For more about tritomas, see the chapter "Pushing the Limits."

Prominent between the torch lilies are groups of true lilies, yellow 'Golden Wedding' and 'Connecticut King' and honey-colored 'Bronze Queen.' All are Asiatic hybrids, a generic name that encompasses many shades and shapes. Lilies ap-

preciate light, well-drained earth and, like alliums, will draw on the reservoir of water in their bulbs during dry times. Flickering through the solid shapes of lilies and tritomas are the tiny white flowers of baby's breath (*Gypsophila paniculata*). Another lover of sun, drainage and lime, baby's breath supports its delicate growth with penetrating roots that tap moisture deep in the soil. After a couple of summers (if all goes well), it billows into a cloud. Three slender bamboo canes pushed in

around a clump and wound with two levels of string encourage the ball of bloom to hover rather than slump. If you have a flourishing gypsophila, resist the urge to move it, and don't even think of dividing it. Such meddling could well be the death of it, as could damp, heavy soil.

The small thistle heads of sea holly, species of *Eryngium*, fill in beautifully among the larger yellow flowers. Ground-hugging leaves are inconsequential, but as stems lengthen and branch out, they grow gradually bluer, ending in sprays of bloom. Actual flowers are so tiny as to be unnoticeable, but they are packed together in heads the size of a hazelnut, each sitting on a ruff of spiky bracts, the whole assembly tinted a curious metallic blue. Eryngiums defy drought by being the opposite of succulent; the whole plant has a prickly, dryish feel. As you might guess, they dry quickly—they are halfway there when you pick them—for winter arrangements. The showiest sea hollies for mass plant-

The Art of Perennial Gardening

great drift of it in the middle row of the Yellow Border. I might yet, but so far, caution prevails.

BACK ROW

Tall-growing perennials are harder to find for a hot, dry site; understandably, the bulkier the plant, the thirstier it is. One for the back row is the aptly named desert candle (*Eremurus stenophyllus* syn. *E. bungei*), its swaying 5-foot (1.5 m) wands ablaze along their top third with yellow star-shaped flowers that fade to rust; at that stage, you understand where their other name, foxtail lily, comes from. Sun and sand are the keys to success with a native of dry, stony land in Turkey and the Middle East. Plant fleshy eremurus roots carefully as soon as they arrive in fall, and situate them where bushy foreground plants will obscure (but not overshadow) their no-account leaves. Some winter protection may be needed to ensure their survival. We've noticed that eremurus roots tend to hoist themselves higher each year until they are so close to the surface, they are in danger of being sliced by hoe or cultivator. When that happens, lift the clump, and ever so gingerly, tease the tangled roots apart into separate crowns for immediate replanting. In time, you will work up a band of glowing desert candles that will draw all eyes in June.

Mulleins figure prominently in the Yellow Border. Most mulleins are biennials, and most are tall and yellow. The showy *Verbascum chaixii* 'Album' is an exception: Solidly perennial and shorter than most mulleins, its purple-centered white blooms are arrayed up tapering stems typical of the family. This is altogether a worthy plant and one that always attracts attention. As mentioned, mulleins share pollen freely, not that they have any choice with bees working their flowers inces-

ing include *E. amethystinum*, *E. planum* and *E. tripartitum*, with the cultivar 'Blaukapp' among the finest. My advice, if you like these weird perennials, is to take a chance with any you come across.

Truly lovely in its silver adornments is *Artemisia* 'Powis Castle,' its finely cut leafage the perfect touch amid the yellows and lavenders. At least for a summer: Sadly, five months crushed under wet snow finished ours off. Some plants can suffer a devastating winter setback only to

start again from a few lively shoots. Not this artemisia; it vanished without a trace. A reliable substitute—our clumps are pushing 20 years—is *A. absinthium* 'Lambrook Silver.' Its filigree may not be as delicately fashioned as 'Powis Castle,' but 'Lambrook Silver' fills out well after a spring trim-up and looks fresh until November if the dull flower stems are cut away in midsummer. The massed gray leaves of *A.* 'Silver King' I always admire in other gardens. If its roots were less aggressive, I would plant a

santly. From all appearances, the shorter white perennial has crossed with a tall yellow biennial. How else to explain the spontaneous appearance of a tall yellow mullein that keeps coming back every year and even submits to careful division? However it came to be, this surprise plant now lives contentedly in the back row of the Yellow Border. One summer, we set some double-flowered 'Apricot' hollyhocks (seed from Thompson and Morgan) next to the mullein. What a tender picture the two made against the rail fence—soft yellow spires entwined with staves of pinky apricot pom-poms—nice enough to change my opinion of double hollyhocks.

Two more half-wild creatures share this back-row space. Tallest of the *Achillea* clan, *A. filipendulina* reaches 4 feet (1.2 m) and enjoys a place in the sun. There are no tricks to growing this noninvasive yarrow, which displays flat mustard-yellow flowerheads for weeks in late summer. Foliage is pleasantly gray-green and nicely cut. This is a perennial you either appreciate for its sturdy constitution and long flowering or dismiss as inelegant, bulky, coarse and wild-looking. We've grown it for almost two decades—but then, we have space to fill.

Wilder yet is the latest introduction to this border—goldenrod. Let's clear up one misconception: Goldenrod does not cause hay fever in most people; the usual culprit is ragweed, a dowdy thing that hides under a plain green camouflage. Even so, North American gardeners are apt to laugh at pictures of English borders alight with masses of goldenrod in late summer. A common query is, Why grow weeds?

I doubt we would have tried goldenrod were it not for the intriguing description of *Solidago* 'Lemore'— "large panicles of primrose yellow." The lighter color intrigued us—it was not the usual mustard of the plumes that jostle with purple asters and white Queen Anne's lace in fall meadows. The verdict after one summer: We like 'Lemore,' a soft touch (the flowers, not us) in both color and texture—not dramatically different from its sibling on the other side of the fence, but at least we know 'Lemore' will live. The fact that goldenrod wants nothing more than "average well-drained soil in sun"—and not a drop of water beyond what falls from the heavens—also endears it.

The Art of Perennial Gardening

FOUNTAINS OF FOLIAGE

ORNAMENTAL GRASSES FOR GRACEFUL EFFECTS

"The value of good foliage cannot be overstated; flowers come and go…"

GRAHAM STUART THOMAS

FACING PAGE: *Variegated miscanthus catches the morning sun beside a dipping pool, while a towering foxtail lily continues the upward line.*

ABOVE: *Striped tuberous oatgrass brings the intense red of 'Paprika' yarrow into sharp relief.*

THE FIRST TIME I SAW JAPANESE SILVER grass, a single clump on the brow of a hill in Toronto's Edwards Gardens, I was immediately taken with its graceful outline, the way its leaves swayed in the breeze, the lively green when so much around was August-spent. "Wouldn't *that* be nice for the garden?" I thought. And that may have been the first time I had ever considered a plant for anything other than its flowers.

Flowers draw many of us to gardening; flowers keep us at it. Witness the trouble taken for delphiniums—the stumbling job of staking, the raising of replacements—for the sake of that peerless blue. But inevitably, the August morning dawns when all the earlier glories are faded (even delphiniums are reduced to ragged leftovers) and the remaining flowers are flying their colors in the midst of general dishevelment. You start making

mental notes (real ones too, if you're smart) of any plants still freshly green or gray or whatever—so long as their leaves count for something at this untidy season. You resolve to grow more foliage plants and shift those you already have into prominent places.

There may be some folks of a more Zen cast who come to gardening with a built-in appreciation for leaves. I admire the austerity and clean lines of a Japanese meditation garden—but not in my backyard. Italian gardens, all green and gravel, fail to move me. A hearty amen to the writer who said, "I continue to feel that a flowerless garden is a sad place." But when the bloom is off, so is a garden planned entirely around flowers. Balance is called for. Grow the flowers you admire, but understand that they will look lovelier in a setting of enduring foliage. Some

perennials do double duty—flowers and lasting leaves—but grasses are grown for their leaves alone.

Once grass was the enemy in our garden, something to dig out and keep out. Not anymore: Each year, I recognize the value of ornamental grasses more. Grasses bring different lines and textures to a garden than flowering perennials do—a kind of lightness, a softening effect. Anyone who has looked over a field of waving wheat (itself a grass) knows something of the appeal. It has to do with motion, the sway and dance and ripple of grasses; with fluidity of line, the way each blade ascends then bends in a graceful arc; and with sound, wind whispering or hissing through the blades, the clatter of stems. And beyond these aesthetic considerations, grasses deserve our attention because they are among the easiest perennials to grow.

FACING PAGE: *Foliage plants such as Japanese silver grass (left) and the giant eulalia grass (right) are important season-long features in our Quiet Garden, along with ordinary cooking sage and reedy Siberian irises beside the pool.*

LEFT: *The graceful lines of variegated miscanthus offset the stiffer swordlike leaves of bearded iris 'Stepping Out.'*

JAPANESE SILVER GRASS

The feathery plumes depicted in traditional Japanese watercolors are the flowers of *Miscanthus sinensis*, native to sunny hillsides in Japan, Taiwan and China. As a group, miscanthus embodies all that is best in garden grasses: elegance, grace, permanence and ease of care. A potential drawback may be its height, since most varieties can grow taller than you. Their eventual girth—as wide as a bushel basket at the base and twice that at the top, where blades arch out—may also be a problem in smaller gardens. On the plus side, they are noninvasive. While some grasses increase by sending runners in all directions, miscanthus widens very gradually, a trait you'll appreciate if you've ever had to untangle grass roots from neighboring flowers.

Currently, Larkwhistle is home to half a dozen cultivars of *Miscanthus sinensis*. The first we tried was the one that caught my eye in the park. In full growth, *M.s.* 'Gracillimus' is very

like a fountain, shooting narrow green leaves to a height of 4 to 6 feet (1.2 to 1.8 m), then flaring at the top to form a symmetrical sheaf. A thin white rib down the center of each blade lends sparkle as the grass moves. Like many tall grasses, miscanthus look at home near water. Beside our Kitchen Garden pool, three clumps of 'Gracillimus,' initially spaced 2 feet (60 cm) apart, now appear like one enormous, impenetrable plant. I almost prefer this grass as a single specimen, its sleek outline visible from top to bottom. With us, 'Gracillimus' has never flowered—cold weather sets in too early for it—but that hardly matters, since its foliage is the thing.

Several cultivars are like 'Gracillimus' except for some important details. 'Sarabande' is shorter and more contained, and its silvery midrib is more pronounced. In our

garden, it sends up fluffy grayish plumes on stiff stems in September and October. Blades of the taller 'Morning Light' have a pencil line of white along their edges, making the grass appear to shimmer when the wind blows. The giant eulalia grass (*Miscanthus* 'Giganteus') is a great bamboolike creature as high as an elephant's eye. Tall and leggy, this imposing grass belongs at the very back of a bed or off in the distance. I find it a bit intimidating close-up. When the wind gets going, its woody stems clatter against each other.

Two more dramatic miscanthus highlight our garden in lovely ways. The blades of *Miscanthus sinensis* 'Variegatus' are painted along their length with green and cream stripes. If I had room for only one, this might be it. Like a beam of light from the earth, its effect is bright and showy. The second, 'Zebrinus,' is unique

among foliage plants: Horizontal bands of yellow decorate its leaves—a length of green, a cross stroke of yellow, and so on, up the blade. Rigid and upright, 'Zebrinus' lacks the graceful flow of other miscanthus but stands alone for its dappled jungly impression—like a Rousseau painting. There just might be some creature lurking in the tall blades of "tiger grass."

As with all grasses, the great virtue of miscanthus lies in the orderly repetition of line, each blade describing a symmetrical arc. Although their presence can be calming in a bed of giddy flowers, placement calls for some thought; badly situated, the big plants look incongruous and awkward. The fact that they resent casual transplanting—we watched an established 'Zebrinus' sulk for two years after being moved—is further inducement to get the right location

FACING PAGE: *Exploding in almost tropical luxuriance, yellow-banded zebra grass shelters clumps of lily of the Nile and contrasts with the lacy caps of a small peegee hydrangea tree in late August.*

LEFT: *Like a beam of light from the ground, variegated miscanthus interrupts the green of cushion spurge (left) and a rugosa rose laden with hips. Even in September, with few flowers in evidence, this trio remains presentable.*

at the start. Careful shifting in the second season, before the grasses are deeply rooted, does little harm.

Here are some siting suggestions. The middle area of an island bed—but not right in the center—is a good place for a single miscanthus. Face it down with robust perennials in the 2-foot (60 cm) range such as 'East Friesland' salvia, 'Moonshine' yarrow, the shorter astilbes, hardy geraniums, 'Autumn Joy' sedum, Lady's mantle and bergenia. For better proportions, use three of a particular perennial in front of one clump of grass. Space the foreground plants 18 inches (45 cm) from each other and from the grass. Such an arrangement works well at the end of a border too, the perennials at the front and the grass behind. But single grass clumps at either end of a border start to look like a pair of bookends.

Miscanthus provides height and a sense of almost tropical lushness in a narrow border between a walkway and a house wall, fence or hedge. Set the grass closer to the backdrop than the path, or you may provoke the resident garden grouch to attack with weedeater or machete, muttering all the while, "What is this thing? How the heck am I supposed to get through here?" In our Quiet Garden, a clump of 'Gracillimus' stands close by a path; there is no way past it without pushing leaves aside—like going through a curtained doorway. John thinks it adds a touch of mystery; I find it irritating.

Miscanthus comes into its own in late summer, after the tide of earlier flowers has ebbed. It associates well with all the late-season "daisies": heleniums, rudbeckias (black-eyed Susans), heliopsis (false sunflowers), yarrows of many kinds and goldenrod (if you've acquired a taste for it). Turn up the wattage among these yellow and copper blooms by choosing the creamy 'Variegatus' or yellow-banded 'Zebrinus' grass. The green and silvery miscanthus enhance pink coneflowers, fall sedum, phlox and astilbes.

In outline, miscanthus are formal and balanced-looking. Dotting them at precise intervals through a border overemphasizes the symmetry (although some gardeners may find such stability welcome). Their height dictates a back-row position—you'd be hard-pressed to find anything taller. But avoid arrangements in which only the top leaves of grass peek over a tall helenium or phlox.

The Art of Perennial Gardening

Drift taller perennials off to the sides and use knee-high plants in the immediate foreground to allow an open sight line to the grass.

I always like to see miscanthus growing beside a post or fence, where the tension between solid, stationary wood and fluid foliage becomes obvious, the vertical line of the post emphasizing the grass's sweeping curves. For reasons I can't quite explain—perhaps because both stir in the gentlest breeze—miscanthus looks lovely by the water. But keep proportions in mind: One clump of grass can easily overshadow a small pool. Purling water, swaying leaves, sibilant breezes through the grass—there's nothing more restorative on a hot summer day.

At Larkwhistle, a favorite perennial picture starts with 'Zebrinus' beside a raised five-sided pool. In front are clumps of both blue and white lily of the Nile (*Agapanthus umbellatus*), a plant pushing well past its normal hardiness limit in this zone (see the chapter "Pushing the Limits"). To one side are the pinkish white lace caps of the common peegee hydrangea (*Hydrangea paniculata* 'Grandiflora'), in this case, a small tree, or standard, form. Pink phlox completes a scene that is all you could ask for in August, a month that sometimes looks tired and spent.

Miscanthus thrive in sun or very light shade in decent loam fed with organic matter. A few spadefuls of compost or old manure mulched over the soil every year should keep them in trim. When several are planted in a group, leave 2 feet (60 cm) between them. In our Kitchen Garden, where the soil has benefited from 20 years of manuring, these grasses grow with startling health and gusto beside the dipping pools. I love to watch them tossing in the wind—rippling, waving, side-streaming. It's amazing how much buffeting they will take and still return to upright composure when the wind calms down.

Many folks appreciate the sight of curled, papery grasses, golden and translucent, backlit by a winter evening's sun. But such a scene presumes light snowfall. Where snow accumulates, grasses (and everything else) are eventually crushed, and picking up the mess in spring is tedious work. Here, we let them stand as late as possible, usually into November, and then reluctantly cut them to the ground, a ritual that marks the season's end.

SEA LYME GRASS

Most of our early horticultural education (and inspiration) came from several old gardening books written between 1916 and 1935. In *Colour in My Garden* (1918), Louise Beebe Wilder lavishes praise on *Elymus arenarius* (syn. *E. glaucus*). "Of gray plants for the border, none is finer than the Sea Lyme Grass....All through the summer and autumn and until snow is on the ground, its strong, grasslike foliage retains the beautiful color, taking its place harmoniously with whatever scheme …is the fashion of the moment in its neighborhood, and outlasting them all."

The search was on. Ten years later, we finally found this grass listed in a specialist's catalog from the United States. So near yet so far: "No shipments outside the U.S." Desperate, we wrote a friend in New Jersey to ask if she would take delivery and forward the plants to us. A few weeks later, two silvery tufts, their bare roots wrapped in moss, arrived in our mailbox in a padded envelope (oh, the lengths to which the obsessed will go). Now, we can't get rid of the blessed thing.

In her enthusiasm, Wilder had forgotten to tell us that this sterling grass spreads underground on long, wiry runners, precisely like the quack grass we had worked so hard to fork out. Today, sea lyme grass is available closer to home and comes with a warning: "Invasive in the extreme." Gertrude Jekyll, turn-of-the-century English garden guru, also applauded this grass ("of much value for blue effects in the garden"), but as one commentator notes, "Her garden staff must have hated it."

There is no denying the special beauty of lyme grass in the garden picture, a yard-high (1 m) silver-blue sea wave curling toward the edge of a bed. Droughtproof and hardy, this wide-leafed grass would be so right in so many places—except for its one nasty habit. Our approach is to allow

FACING PAGE: *The strong magenta of some phloxes can be hard to companion, but silver sea lyme grass and a blur of blue aconite in the background can successfully create a feeling of harmony.*

LEFT: *Effective at the edge of a bed, sea lyme grass, here with Lady's mantle, is literally curbed by an unseen concrete edging in front; still, its roots may need annual restraining.*

The Art of Perennial Gardening

roots to run for a season, then we hack, dig and pull them into bounds in spring and let them take off again. Extra work, to be sure, but nothing is as fine fringing the lower stems of leggy shrubs or spraying up beside a pool. We seem to have two kinds: One sends up straight stalks of tan grain above the arching blades; the other never flowers.

Magenta—"a little purple mixed with red"—can be an awkward color

to companion, and nothing soothes it into harmony as well as gray leaves. In our garden, sea lyme grass nestles beside a no-name phlox of piercing magenta and stands behind the strongly magenta *Geranium sanguineum*. It once consorted with the now outlawed loosestrife. Needless to say, there is no trick to growing this grass. Plant it, and stand back. In heavier soils, it spreads more slowly but is harder to dig out.

TUBEROUS OATGRASS

Burdened with the cumbersome Latin name *Arrhenatherum elatius bulbosum* 'Variegatum' is a sweet 18-inch (45 cm) grass that we'd better call by its dull, easy English name: tuberous oatgrass. Underground, you'll find a mass of tan, pea-sized balls packed together, tubers from which sprout narrow blades pin-striped in green and white. The effect is fresh and cheerful from early spring until sometime in July if the summer is dry. When the lawn turns brown and strawlike, so does this grass. At this stage, we usually take the scissors to it for a quick brush cut. In a month, it rebounds and stays presentable into November. You could do worse than six months of attractive foliage.

This is one grass that looks better in groups of three or more spaced 1 foot (30 cm) apart at the front of a bed. For earlier color, we stud the ground all around with snow crocuses, chionodoxa and other small spring bulbs. As long as it sees the sun for most of the day, oatgrass flourishes in any soil. Along the front of our sun-baked Yellow Border, a patch of oatgrass is a cooling presence. On one side stands the silver-and-lemon 'Moonshine' yarrow and on the other the dusty green pebbled leaves and lavender flower spikes of 'Blue Wonder' catmint. In another bed, red 'Paprika' yarrow burns all the brighter in contrast with the light-

colored oatgrass. Elsewhere, the grass blends quietly with white flowers. Like sea lyme grass, oatgrass harmonizes with any color.

Often we press this adaptable grass into service where some plant has died over winter. Dividing oat-

grass into smaller pieces for replanting is a most simple matter. In early spring, as soon as new leaves start to bristle through last year's stubble, fork a clump out of the ground and break it apart by hand (if it doesn't fall to bits first). Aim for saucer-sized chunks, and tuck them in wherever you need fresh plants. In a few weeks, the area will be nicely refreshed. How useful—a noninvasive medium-height plant that can be split up and spread around, with immediate results almost guaranteed.

MOOR GRASS

Yellow-and-green stripes decorate the narrow, arching leaves of the 2-foot (60 cm) variegated moor grass, *Molinia caerulea* 'Variegata.' The overall effect is more cream than green. Pale stems carry flowerheads whiskered with purplish anthers that contrast with the foliage below. Widening slowly, this hardy, no-nonsense grass takes care of itself in the same spot for years. Division is possible but seldom necessary.

For the most part, I'm indifferent to yellow-leafed plants; they always look a bit starved or jaundiced, and I can't shake the association between yellow foliage and disease. But moor grass has a vibrancy that keeps it from looking sickly. Useful for edging, it retains color while the showier oatgrass takes a midsummer siesta. By November, it has faded to a ghost of its summer self, its leaves the color and texture of old paper. According to one English commentator, this parchment phase is "conspicuously beautiful in the winter sunlight." I wouldn't know. Here, the winter sun plays on sparkling snowfields. Moor grass, though, is one of the few plants we do not cut back in fall. Winter flattens it. Come spring, after a drying week or two, we take a few minutes to gather up the strawy remnants of last year's leaves, either by hand or with a springy leaf rake.

In a rock raised bed around our front porch, seven clumps of moor grass, spaced a foot (30 cm) apart, are interplanted with yellow Asiatic lilies. The bed is high and dry. A sunny picture for little effort, the lilies and grasses return faithfully every year—never mind that they're a bit stunted in the lean earth. Moor grass will put up with extreme cold, a range of soils and general neglect. Of several types of *Molinia*, the variegated form is the most decorative. The all-green one looks like something you would dig out if it didn't have a name tag beside it.

RIBBON GRASS

This is one of the few grasses commonly found in older farm-country gardens. A "grandmother's plant" like hollyhocks and sweet William, it was making the rounds in rural areas

long before the current enthusiasm for perennial gardening and grasses took root. As you'd expect, it goes by many names: ribbon grass, gardener's garters, striped grass, daggers, ladies' lace, bride's lace and snake grass. The botanically minded call it *Phalaris arundinacea*. If you live in the country and are on friendly terms with neighbors, you won't need to buy ribbon grass. A few roots from an old clump, and you're on your way.

Stripes and variegations abound among ornamental grasses—probably because most plain green grasses look like the stuff of lawns and hayfields. The blades of ribbon grass are particolored green, cream and white, the stripe width varying from leaf to leaf. This fresh-looking 4-foot (1.2 m) grass does well almost anywhere. In wet places, where the creeping rootstock weaves it into a close ground cover, it grows especially lush. Those

same roving roots may pose a problem in small gardens.

Taller grasses are effectively companioned with bold-leafed perennials such as bergenia, Lady's mantle, geraniums or any of the big-leafed heucheras. In our Quiet Garden, ribbon grass is in a constant shoving match with self-sowing sweet Cicely and rampaging lamium. Such pushy neighbors help curb the grass's roots, but the fountain of foliage surges through. Elsewhere, this grass is in subtle contrast with the hoary light maroon leaves of *Rosa rubrifolia*, a 7-foot (2 m) shrub rose. We have a sentimental attachment to ribbon grass, one of the stalwarts we found in the tangle when we came to this old farm site. The similar *Miscanthus* 'Variegatus' may be the better plant, but history and a proven track record keep a clump of old-fashioned gardener's garters with us.

FACING PAGE: *Because it runs from the root, old-fashioned ribbon grass needs careful placement; robust perennials such as sweet Cicely and lamium can withstand the encroachment.*

LEFT: *Low-key and bristly, blue oatgrass contrasts with the broad leaves of the equally subdued salvia 'Berggarten,' inviting a creative gardener to add color.*

BLUE OATGRASS

In just two seasons, blue oatgrass (*Helictotrichon sempervirens*) has proven itself both useful and beautiful. To that description, add care-free: So far, we have not done a thing for it except a bit of cleanup—a trim and a fluff—in spring. Until snow flies and beyond, this tidy, symmetrical grass remains in good form, a quiet companion to fleeting flowers around it. *Sempervirens* means evergreen or, in this case, everblue. A fellow gardener tells me that blue oatgrass breaks apart easily for propagation in early spring, but even though I need more of this easy-care grass for a problem spot, I'm reluctant to disturb our single clump for fear of ruining a good thing. Whether I'm more reluctant to spend the money on five new plants remains to be seen.

At roughly 2 feet (60 cm) tall and wide, blue oatgrass fits in nicely at the front of a sunny bed. I would hesitate to plant anything too close that might detract from the grass's simple lines and refined look. Instead, I picture it facing down peonies and Siberian irises, adjacent to hardy geraniums or shading the lower stems of pink lilies.

Almost by accident—we had no other spot for it—we companioned this grass with a new sage, *Salvia officinalis* 'Berggarten,' a broad-leafed version of ordinary cooking sage. The marked contrast between smooth, straight, silvery grass and rounded, rough-surfaced, dusty green sage works well. When deep violet and mauve bearded irises broke into bloom nearby, the trio sang ever so nicely. You have to appreciate hardy, simple plants like these, which give so much pleasure and ask for so little attention in return.

The Art of Perennial Gardening

PUSHING
THE LIMITS

GROWING PERENNIALS BEYOND THEIR ZONE

*"Few things are more annoy-
ing than dogmatism; and
dogmatism is nowhere more
misplaced than in horticulture."*
Reginald Farrer

FACING PAGE: *The tiny honey-scented
florets of buddleia—the butterfly bush—
feed butterflies winging south in fall.*

ABOVE: *Perhaps hardier than once
supposed, airy white crambe hovers
over the garden in early summer.*

WINTER IS A GARDEN'S ROUGHEST PASSAGE, a grueling trial by ice and snow; worse yet, extreme cold followed by beguiling mild spells more menacing than a steady deep freeze. Pity the poor confused perennials, roused again and again by unseasonable wake-up calls. No wonder some of them perish. After a while, you grow philosophical about winter losses— they are bound to happen. You may even begin to see the gaps left by dead daisies or lavender bushes as opportunities to try something new. But real gardeners never quite learn to play it safe.

Says Graham Stuart Thomas in his useful book, *Perennial Garden Plants*: "It is a strange characteristic of gardeners…that they always try to achieve success with plants which are not quite hardy in their gardens." And why not? You expend a few dollars and half an hour's work, cross your fingers and wait. With a little luck, some marginally tender perennial will squeak through, and "in the resulting triumph, a great satisfaction lies" (again Thomas). You've proven the experts, naysayers and hardiness maps wrong. Gazing on a clump of tropical-looking crocosmia or agapanthus in full flower, gardening friends will praise your skill and admire your chutzpah for leaving them in the ground year-round.

Gardening, someone once said, is the art of touching up nature. It is also an act of challenging nature, outwitting the elements and pushing beyond the limitations of your immediate environment. In the process, though, a healthy dose of realism saves a lot of work, waste and frustration. As much as I'd love to see a star magnolia, for example, spreading its white-wreathed boughs over a bed of spring bulbs or watch a wisteria wend its way over an arbor, I'm not so foolish as to throw away $35 on a project doomed to fail the first winter. I will, however, concoct a special pocket of soggy, acidic soil—lots of

peat, leaf mold and a few handfuls of sulfur—in our sandy, lime-filled garden in hopes of winning over a Japanese iris. I'm also prepared to thwart Old Man Winter by laying down a 'New Dawn' rose each October, covering it completely with earth and then resurrecting the thorny climber six months later for the sake of those fragrant, pale pink blooms in July. And I do not always take hardiness ratings as gospel truth.

Every garden needs a touch of exotica, every gardener a challenge.

In our zone-4 garden grow a handful of perennials that by all accounts should not be alive after a winter this far north. One fall, a visitor brought a handful of montbretia bulbs, which we planted first and read about afterward. "Native to South Africa, zone 6-10," said the reference books. So much for montbretia. What a surprise, then, to see the pointed blades emerge in spring. A decade later, montbretia—now called crocosmia—is still going strong. We try other tender perennials knowing the odds are against us. Torch lilies and *Lavatera* 'Barnsley' look so enticing; maybe a winter mounding or mulch would see them through.

Pushing the limits of hardiness is an exercise fraught with potential failure. On the other hand, I'd have nothing to tell you if a number of so-called tender plants had not proven their mettle over the years in our garden. What follows might qualify as bragging—I wouldn't be the first gardener to flaunt successes—except for the fact that we've done very little to win over these marginal beauties. The particularities of our soil and site help a lot. Be bold, experiment, run a trial. Who knows, some southern belle may put down roots and stay.

LILY OF THE NILE

To begin with the one that first surprised us—"shocked" would be more like it—by proving to be perennial far away from its balmy zone-8-to-10 home: lily of the Nile (*Agapanthus umbellatus*), also known as blue African lily. The botanical name comes from the Greek *agape*, love, and *anthos*, flower. A lovely flower, to be sure, but the common names suggest hot summers and inconsequential winters. This is an altogether elegant plant, from its fountain of simple leaves to the small, clustered, clear blue or white trumpet flowers arranged in loose bunches on 2-foot (60 cm) stems. Agapanthus is offered in spring along with "tender summer bulbs"—gladiolus, dahlias, and such. The usual recommendation is to plant the fleshy roots in an oversized container, enjoy the peerless blue on the deck in summer, haul the container into a cool, dry place for the winter and start over in spring. Alternatively, plant in the ground in May, enjoy the blue flowers in August, and dig up for winter storage like any glad or dahlia. After trying both methods and enjoying not a scrap of blue, we gave up on expert advice.

Method three was a long shot. We would leave the roots in the ground year-round. If they made it through the winter, fine; if not, *adieu*. Not being cruel gardeners, we mounded three buckets of sandy soil over the place where agapanthus was to live (or not, as the case might be) through the cold months. Imagine the thrill the following May when, carefully pawing away the mound of cool earth, we found not mush but perky blanched leaf tips clearly ready to grow. By August, several bud-topped stems had risen up, and when the blue blossoms broke open in the company of mauve phlox and a small peegee hydrangea tree draped with pink-white lace, we thought the goddess Flora had done us an exceptional favor. Given the same mounding treatment in November, the original three plants returned the next spring and the next. Now, a decade later, a proper fat clump of agapanthus, like any tough old daylily, has formed. Which leaves us in a pleasant quandary: Do we disturb a plant that has grown overcrowded instead of dying as predicted, or do we leave well enough alone?

As I see it, there are three secrets to the success of this African perennial in our winter-blasted garden. First, the soil is sandy and very well drained. Autumn rains flow through, leaving no water pooled around roots. Cold, soggy ground would surely prove fatal. Second, the foot-high (30 cm) mound of earth offers a slight but crucial bit of extra protection. Third—and most important—snow begins to fall early, piling up into a deep duvet, drifting even higher in the lee of the rail fences, shrubs and evergreens that shelter our garden from icy winds. Under the snow, the earth often remains unfrozen—cold and slightly damp, but not frozen. As it happens, this is precisely the environment recommended for the winter storage of many tender tubers, roots and bulbs.

The Art of Perennial Gardening

mulch, and think deep: piles of leaves or burlap sacks stuffed with leaves, a heavy thatch of straw, a giant anthill of manure, compost or peat. Whatever material is used, it must not only rise to a considerable height over the roots but extend out some distance. The goal is (not so simply) to keep the ground where agapanthus is growing from freezing, a major—perhaps an impossible—task where frost extends deep into the earth all around. The surprise can only be pleasant: If agapanthus dies on you, well, that could have been predicted; if it lives and flowers, now *that* will be wonderful.

BEAR'S BREECHES

The imposing bear's breeches is with us entirely by accident—thanks to lax labeling at a nursery. One spring, in the process of renovating a perennial bed, we set a trio of what we thought were globe thistles in the second-row position. As the small plants grew—and grew—it became obvious that they had been incorrectly tagged. Instead of the expected spiny, gray-green foliage, enormous jagged, dark green leaves—like some monstrous dandelion—arched up and out, obliterating hapless small plants in front. By July, the greenery had piled up waist-high, and from its midst emerged prickly, pointed clubs, 5 feet (1.5 m) tall and set with fat buds. These in turn developed into pinkish white hooded flowers, each overhung with a dusky plum awning ending in a sharp barb. Curiouser and curiouser. Back to the books we went, only to discover that we were the proud (if perplexed) owners of a thriving patch of *Acanthus spinosus*, or bear's breeches, a native of Sicily, Spain, Portugal and North Africa—zones 7 to 10. A spectacular novelty for a summer, we concluded; the mistake could be rectified next spring. Except that next spring, those same big, jagged leaves came back. So far,

Even a foot (30 cm) of snow is enough to insulate the ground against temperature fluctuations above.

Indeed, it might be said that our garden lies in two hardiness zones when blanketed by snow: zone 4 above the snow and zone 6 or better at ground level. The same wind-chilled air that deals death to marginally hardy shrubs exposed to the heavens cannot extend its grip into the ground. These few quirks of site, soil and climate (conditions no doubt shared by many other gardeners) have enabled us to grow perennials that are routinely winter-killed farther south. Encouraged by the performance of blue agapanthus, we planted a white one beside it. Same treatment, same outcome. Knock on wood.

Always site agapanthus in the sun in well-drained earth; lighten heavy clay with lots of sand and compost. In areas with less dependable snow cover, more protection will be needed to bring agapanthus successfully through the winter outdoors. Think

FACING PAGE: *Expert opinion to the contrary, bear's breeches may settle in beyond the expected zones. The exotic plant stands in bold contrast to the equally prickly rugosa rose 'Mrs. Anthony Waterer.'*

LEFT: *Where space allows, sprawling bear's breeches might accompany more ordinary summer residents such as daylilies, lilies and lavender.*

bear's breeches has made it through five winters with no signs of stress or damage.

Much as I appreciate the hardiness and strength of bear's breeches—you would need a thick hide to wear breeches cut from such rough cloth—I cannot say I am enamored of it. Big, sharp-toothed, pushy, it is not the friendliest plant in the garden. A well-armored, stand-alone thing, it does not invite closeness or touch—lamb's ears or baby's breath it is not. And we had planted them near the edge of a bed where the head-high plants are most defiantly, as they say, in your face. I do feel mollified, though, by the sentiments of one authority who writes of acanthus: "Their leaves are so handsome that they are most appreciated in frontal positions, where there is enough space, in spite of their floral height." Often the tall spikes will topple over during a windy rainstorm and then continue to grow upward, looking quite natural—and not so domineering—at their diminished height. The

The Art of Perennial Gardening

same expert goes on to say, "Any fertile soil suits them so long as it is reasonably well drained, and they are best planted in the spring and protected by a mulch for the first winter in cold districts or until thoroughly established."

Good drainage and lots of sunshine are the norm in our garden. But since the district certainly qualifies as cold compared to Italy, we protect acanthus for the winter by heaping a foot (30 cm) of earth over the crowns in late October. Given such treatment, it has gone from strength to strength, has been divided successfully and shows every sign of staying. Maybe I'll learn to appreciate acanthus's prickly charms. Old books use expressions like "statuesque" and "classical dignity" to refer to acanthus, and all say that its foliage provided ancient Greek sculptors with a kind of template for the stylized leaf shapes that adorn the tops of Corinthian columns. Far be it from me to argue with a 3,000-year-old aesthetic. Besides, almost all of our visitors are fascinated by this imposing perennial.

As for company for this prickly Italian, I cannot say what would be suitable. I read that in Italy, acanthus seldom has flowery neighbors because flowerbeds are not a feature of Italian gardens. Few perennials are tall enough to peek over acanthus, and anything planted in front would obscure the view of those noble leaves. Phlox or daylilies off to the sides might work, but it has been suggested that "the place for acanthus should be special, a bed of its own, where it can be viewed from all sides, or a place of emphasis at the bottom of a statue or the corner of a path or at the foot of a wall." Talk of walls and grand statues lets you know that the source of the suggestions is English (Robin Lane Fox, *Variations on a Garden*), and the imagined gardens are big. But the hints are valid: If you like acanthus, give it room of its own. I think the smaller end of a kidney-

shaped island bed would be appropriate, and I would plant some early daffodils all around for spring color—and stand back.

TORCH LILIES

I forget when we first planted torch lilies. At the time, we called them *Tritoma*, a name that rolls off the tongue more readily than the current *Kniphofia* (pronounced knee-*foe*-fee-ah). In any case, it was an experiment prompted (as was so much of

our gardening in the early years) by the enthusiasm of the 1920s writer Louise Beebe Wilder, who gardened in Upstate New York in conditions very much like our own and wrote: "I am extravagantly fond of Torch Lilies…used in gracious combination with the hardy plants and annuals of their season. The flaming scarlets, warm coral reds and golden apricots of the torches are in fine harmony or bold contrast with all the autumn flowers, save those that wear the pinkish magenta tones." Wilder paints a picture of "the great flower-heads…piercing a haze of lavender Michaelmas Daisies" accompanying late blue aconites, white Japanese anemones, lavender joe-pye weed and white phlox.

Torch lilies—the name describes the elongated heads of small, down-facing, tubular flowers—are natives of southern Africa; their hardiness is listed as zone 6 and southward, with the occasional variety tough enough to winter in zone 5. Intrigued by Wilder's description, we set one plant at the end of a vegetable bed in spring, hoping to see flowers that fall but resigned to losing the plant over winter—an oddball annual. Sure enough, come September, several exotic-looking 3-foot (1 m) tapers materialized. In ascending order, red buds opened into yellow-orange flowers, a glowing coloration, like burning embers, that immediately made sense of the plant's other name, redhot poker.

As with many marginally hardy perennials, winter wet can be as damaging as cold. All experts advise binding up the foliage of torch lilies in fall and leaving it in place over winter as a water-shedding tent. Dutifully, but without much hope of success, we bunched and tied the long, thin leaves. Winter howled in and melted out. And, once again, a supposedly tender plant made a surprising comeback. A decade later, our first torch lily is still in place, hale and obviously hardier than described.

Soil plays an important role in getting kniphofias through the winter. Take heed of the warning that they "dislike wet feet"; roots must have perfect drainage year-round. In addition to sandy ground and a sunny site, a constant snow blanket keeps them cozy during the coldest months. A mound of light soil heaped over their crowns and a generous leaf mulch placed around—but not over—the plants protect torch lilies where snow is hit-and-miss; that

and the current year's foliage tied up in a ponytail. A strange winter sight: a doughnut of leaves around an anthill with a tuft of bedraggled foliage sticking out the top. I have to say that we have become cocky and now simply leave the foliage in place, untied, for snow to flatten—no mounding, no leaf mulch. In spring, the soggy mat is cut and pulled away. I always feel a flutter of relief when I see new shoots poking through. Kniphofias keep you waiting, though; settle into a northern garden they may, but they remain African plants that need a touch of warmth to draw them out.

Kniphofias are not widely available—you take what you find and hope for hardiness. Recently I added three tufts of 'Primrose Beauty,' reputed to be "hardy over a wide area," to a border decked out in yellows, blues, white and silver. A change from the typical redhot pokers, the light yellow spires form a dramatic focal point in August in com-

pany with steel-blue sea holly, tall yellow mulleins, fluffy lemon solidago and airy baby's breath; the silver leaves of yarrow and lamb's ears complete the picture. Over four years, this perennial has not only survived but has increased appreciably.

The Art of Perennial Gardening

Once—or maybe *if*—they settle in, kniphofias grow lovelier with the passing years. Division is neither necessary nor desirable unless they appear to be in decline; weaker growth and fewer torches are the signs. Spring is the only time to tamper. Lift a clump, shake or wash away some of the soil, and carefully cut between the clustered crowns and down through the roots. Replant the liveliest portions in soil fed with some very old manure or fine compost. Allow 2 feet (60 cm) of clear area all around each specimen. The tallish stems make torch lilies ideal for midborder, where their simple grassy foliage, much like a daylily's, remains fresh from May to October. The various cultivars bloom over a span of two months, the first appearing in July with lilies, others waiting until August, and several lighting up the autumn. Of all the marginal perennials, tritomas appear to be the hardiest and may be the safest bet for a trial beyond the usual limits.

CRAMBE CORDIFOLIA

"What is it?" people will ask. "The leaves look like rhubarb, but the flowers are more baby's breath—except it's so *tall*." I can find no common name for a perennial that every year, in late June and early July, hovers like an enormous white cloud 5 feet (1.5 m) off the ground at the edge of our asparagus patch. Which is where we tucked a small seedling of *Crambe cordifolia* on the assumption that this zone-6 native of the Caucasus would probably not survive. Once again, we underestimated a plant's will to live.

Related to cabbage, turnips and radishes, crambe is a member of the family Cruciferae. If you've ever seen a radish run to seed, you know the typical cross-shaped, four-petaled white flowers of the family. What sets crambe apart from the rest of its relatives is the sheer number of flowers—possibly thousands—strung along a complex network of delicate stems that interlace to form a voluminous head, expansive but ever so light. At ground level are great green elephant-ear leaves on thick stalks that resemble rhubarb.

Described as "a deeply rooted plant for rough, well-drained soil in full sun," this impressive perennial is pleased enough with our sandy garden to regrow year after year. The slightly cooler summers and snowbound winters seem to suit it. Lately, seedlings have popped up, a sure sign of contentment (and an indication that seed might be the best way to bring crambe into the garden, especially in the absence of available

FACING PAGE: *Veritable hummingbird feeders, scarlet crocosmias grow from spring-planted corms and contribute their exotic blooms in late summer. In the absence of snow, a heavy mulch should ensure their survival over winter.*

LEFT: *Bulky but ethereal, Crambe cordifolia hangs like a cumulus cloud above violet delphiniums and lighter peach-leaved bellflowers. Three stout bamboo canes and several levels of string keep the cloud airborne.*

plants). When the flower stems are half-grown, we push three tall bamboo canes around the clump and encircle it with strands of twine at several levels to keep the cloud in the air where it belongs. How lovely crambe looks after a summer shower, the sun glinting through beads of water clinging to its flowers and all along the wiry stems. A dark violet delphinium and a few stems of burgundy lilies in front add depth and drama to the scene.

I heard of one Oakville, Ontario, gardener so taken with crambe that she simply had to grow one—even though it fills her entire yard when in bloom. An expansive plant, crambe will brook no crowding. Give it room to round out its cloud and room for the mass of oversized leaves. Three feet (1 m) of space all around is about right for one plant. Last June, when crambe was at its height of glory, I stood at a distance and put up my hand to block it from view. In a moment, I missed the height, the delicacy, the flutter of small petals. That

The Art of Perennial Gardening

must be crambe's appeal: such a big, bulky plant and yet so airy and ethereal. Let's hope it keeps coming back.

CROCOSMIA

If someone hadn't given us a handful of crocosmia bulbs years ago, we would probably still be unacquainted with a perennial that has become one of the finest features of the August garden. "These are supposed to be tender," a bulb-bearing visitor told us one September day, "but I've had them for years—and your winter can't be any worse than mine." The bulbs looked like crocuses—small, round, encased in a fibrous brown husk. Our visitor called them montbretia, and so did we until crocosmia sank in as the correct current name. The Greek *krokos* means saffron, *osme* means smell; as they dry, crocosmia flowers take on the scent of saffron. Crocosmia and crocus—source of real saffron—are cousins, related under the broad banner of Iridaceae, the iris family.

Crocosmias of various kinds are native to South Africa, their hardiness range listed as zone 6 and southward. Time would tell if they had a hope this far north. When daffodils and hyacinths were being planted, the montbretia bulbs were tucked into a sunny out-of-the-way spot in sandy soil. In spring, *mirabile dictu*, pale spears emerged and grew rapidly into slender arching leaves, knee-high, yellow-green and as lovely as any ornamental grass. August brought a succession of graceful stems set with teardrop-shaped red buds that opened into small, pendant, six-petaled, tubular blooms, the back of the petals reddish orange, the inside apricot with a necklace of tiny red dots at the throat. "Hummingbird feeders," I thought, before seeing the first rubythroats flash and hover.

From all appearances, this plant seems to match the description of *Crocosmia* x *crocosmiiflora*, a hardier hybrid that was developed by Lemoine in the late 1800s in France. The warm-toned flowers belong in sunny beds with Shasta daisies, yellow heliopsis, blue globe thistles or sea hollies and late lilies in the yellow, orange and red range. 'Heart's Desire' lily—white curled-back petals and a yellow throat with a sprinkling of cinnamon dots—is always handsome company.

Over the years, our first few crocosmias have multiplied with such zeal—they have actually sent out underground runners like those of quack grass, strung with increasing numbers of new bulbs—that we have been able to split them time and again to make new patches. Nothing could be better—and, surprisingly, few plants have proven as permanent—for the edge of a sunny bed than a generous group of this exotic perennial. Sunlight and shadow play beautifully among the grassy leaves as they move in the breeze. For some reason, men in particular seem to be drawn to this plant; it is almost always a man who asks about it, and those who do seem mesmerized by the way the light darts and dances among the blades. Maybe the jungle foliage speaks to their inner Tarzan or something.

Encouraged by our initial experience—and having seen a spectacular clump of crocosmia 'Lucifer' in full blaze in a Stratford, Ontario, garden—we sent away for the few cultivars listed in a spring catalog with "summer bulbs." Although rated as hardy to zone 6 (or "zone 5 with mulch"), all have survived three winters so far with no protection beyond a thick snow cover; all have increased appreciably. 'Lucifer' is the standout (and quite different from the others). Wide, dark green leaves rise up straight and tall to a height of more than a yard (meter), like a strong-growing gladiolus. One writer aptly describes them: "Broad, swordlike foliage in beauty all summer." From their midst come arching branched stems studded with upturned freesia-like blooms of burning scarlet, a color to draw all eyes. As perennials go, 'Lucifer' is a relative newcomer, bred by English plantsman Alan Bloom of Bressingham Gardens fame in 1979 and rated as "one of [his] best efforts." A well-placed clump of 'Lucifer' brings a sense of freshness and order to the garden during the late-summer weeks I think of as the "glorious mess" phase—seedy, tangled, colorful and heading for fall.

With us, 'Lucifer' blooms beside *Artemisia lactiflora* 'Guizho' (another Bressingham introduction), a tall plant with sprays of tiny cream-white blooms similar to astilbe's that hover above purple-black stems and dark ferny leaves. To elaborate the picture where space permits, add a few clumps of monkshood—blue-and-white, deep violet or ivory—behind 'Lucifer,' and face down the artemisia with late orange or yellow daylilies. There is nothing subtle about the flashing interplay of scarlet, orange, blue and cream, a bold display for those who adore intense color.

One perennial reference book lists over 20 crocosmia cultivars—variations on a theme of yellow, orange and red. Good luck finding three or four from local sources. Recent breeding work has improved hardiness,

but even so, frozen ground means dead bulbs. Varieties range from 2 to 4 feet (60 cm to 1.2 m) tall. Plant crocosmias in spring, 3 inches (8 cm) deep and 8 inches (20 cm) apart in drained soil in the sun. Do not expect great things the first summer. Mulch heavily with leaves, dry peat, sawdust or the equivalent in November where snow is unreliable; remove the mulch when the danger of a deep freeze is past—mid-April with us. See that no bulky perennials overshadow the spot where crocosmias grow; I prefer a front-row position for even the tall 'Lucifer.' Should fortune smile on you and your crocosmia patch grow thick and overcrowded, fork the entire clump out of the ground in early spring, and replant the bulbs, giving them space to spread again. Pass the extras along to gardening friends—whoever brought us those first bulbs, thank you.

LAVATERA 'BARNSLEY'

It is easy enough to be seduced by pictures. Sometimes a plant lives up to its catalog portrait; sometimes the blooming reality is a pale semblance of a touched-up photo. A close-up of *Lavatera thuringiaca* 'Barnsley' enticed us to spend a not inconsiderable sum on three plants, despite the caution that this hollyhock relative would be hardy in zone 5 only in a "sheltered location" and wanted "a heavy winter mulch." Other less optimistic (or more realistic) references place this perennial in zones 6 to 10.

There is something so appealing about the simple funnel-shaped flower that characterizes hollyhocks and many of its cousins: hibiscus, mallows, perennial lavateras and the gorgeous annual lavatera known as 'Silver Cup.' Their five heart-shaped petals flare out, and a prominent

fuzzy pistil surrounded by a halo of deeper color around a green star—segments of calyx peeking through gaps in the petals—draws you into the flower's center. *Lavatera* 'Barnsley' fits the pattern; it also holds true to the group's cool, light pink coloring.

Our three new 'Barnsley' lavateras (pronounced lava-*tear*-ah; tear as in rip, not weep) were planted in spring, 18 inches (45 cm) apart at the corner of a stone-faced garden shed. In front was a mass of *Monarda* 'Marshall's Delight,' a lovely deep pink and apparently mildewproof bergamot developed by a Canadian hybridizer. Lavender pincushion flowers (*Scabiosa caucasica*), lilac phlox and white lilies stood in the same field of view with *Veronica* 'Red Fox' (actually deep pink) at the edge. If 'Barnsley' proved a dud, we would have a picture nonetheless; if it failed to make it through the winter, we'd still manage to have plenty of backup bloom.

Neither dud nor dead: Willowy lavatera stems shot up to 5 feet (1.5 m), branched out and unfurled a succession of small funnels from July into September. Delicate in texture and shading, curiously, they opened almost white and "faded" to light pink. Leaning into the bergamot, *Lavatera* 'Barnsley' picked up its rosy tone and conferred on that corner of the garden the informal, cottagey aspect which comes when simple, wild-looking flowers are allowed to spread and sprawl (within reason—a fine line separates controlled untidiness from an inglorious mess). Instead of lilac phlox, I would prefer deep wine to add richness and harmonious contrast.

October came. Knowing that this lavatera, in common with other tree mallows and some hibiscus, can resprout strongly from the base, we treated 'Barnsley' as if it were a tender rose bush, heaping an 18-inch (45 cm) mound of light earth around and over the crown of each plant. Full of curiosity the following April, we gently tickled away the soil to find pale shoots already sprouting beneath the protective mound. Exposed to light, they soon greened up and regrew, repeating the previous year's performance. The second season, some mottled yellow patches appeared on the leaves. Lavatera, like hollyhock, is susceptible to various fungal ailments, more so here because it is wedged tightly between an ever widening stand of bergamot and a stone wall, out of the path of fresh-air circulation. But since most of the plant is obscured and only the tall, flowery wands show, spotty leaves matter little.

Besides phlox, late lilies and pink bergamot, additional company for *Lavatera* 'Barnsley' might include *Eryngium planum*, tall white baby's breath or the shorter 'Rosy Veil,' purple coneflowers and annuals such as cosmos or gladiolus chosen to match.

BUDDLEIA

With the wave of interest in flowers that attract butterflies and hummingbirds to the garden, buddleia—or butterfly bush—is enjoying a spell of popularity. As its common name indicates, the plant is not a herbaceous perennial but a woody bush or shrub; a shrub, that is, where winters are gentle. North of zone 6, all of buddleia's top growth may well be killed by winter, leaving the bush to rebound from the base. Most gardeners understand this pattern and know what to do when it comes to tender roses. Heap soil around the base in fall, remove soil in spring, cut dead branches back to a point below where you see new shoots sprouting. For the effort, I would rather have a buddleia and butterflies than a tender rose and worms. By mid-August, the 4-to-5-foot (1.2 to 1.5 m) buddleia stems should be displaying their cones of violet, purple, wine or white honey-scented flowers—hundreds of tiny tubular blooms packed into heads like elongated lilacs.

Given their habit of growth, buddleias fit in nicely with other perennials, their late-summer flowering helping to refresh beds past their peak. Several cultivars—'Nanho Blue' and 'Nanho Purple,' for two—sport silver foliage that shines all season among the usual greens. 'Black Knight' blooms burgundy; 'Pink Delight' and 'White Profusion' are self-descriptive; other named varieties are worth trying. They are often sold potted in spring.

In a 4-foot-wide (1.2 m) bed down the middle of our Old Garden, a single 'Nanho Blue'—like many "blue" flowers, it is really lavender—blooms in August beside a mass of vibrant magenta phlox. A few wine cosmos volunteer nearby, and down the way is a mass of thistly silver-blue sea holly (*Eryngium* 'Blaukappe'). Clumps of *Sidalcea* 'Party Girl,' their small mauve blooms like scaled-

FACING PAGE: *Cut back hard every spring, butterfly bush returns like any perennial and flowers in August with the candy-floss panicles of queen-of-the-prairie, wine cosmos, double Shasta daisies and delicate baby's breath.*

down hollyhocks growing up thin 3-foot (1 m) stems, sprout beside the sea holly; these are interspersed with lavender miniature gladiolus, the corms tucked into any bare ground in April. When the sky-reaching branches of *Thalictrum* 'Hewitt's Double,' one of the best meadow rues, hang out their little lilac balls, this bed presents such a fresh and colorful aspect, with not a scrap of yellow or orange in sight, you'd think

the year had reverted to June if it weren't for the fall aster budding in the midst of everything.

As drought-tolerant sun lovers, buddleias are naturals for our open, sandy site. Somehow they eluded our curiosity for two decades, but once planted, they quickly joined the ranks of favorite flowers—showy, fragrant and apparently care-free (unless some major problem is waiting in the wings). Besides sunshine

and well-drained, moderately fertile ground, buddleias need some lime in the earth—their wild antecedents grow in chalky or lime soil in the highlands of China and have naturalized on chalk cliffs and among the limestone rubble of bombed-out buildings in Europe. Flowering best on new growth, they should be pruned back hard every spring; as mentioned, winter will probably do much of the pruning for you. Buddleia has an informal habit, a polite way of saying that its branches spray out in all directions and at all angles, often growing through adjacent plants and using them as support.

THE BLUE POPPY

I'm almost reluctant to write about the blue poppy (*Meconopsis betonicifolia*) for fear of jinxing the blessed thing. By all accounts, this Himalayan wildflower is tricky, miffy and just plain temperamental in lowland gardens. If it lives, you count yourself favored by the goddess Flora. In English gardens, the silken flowers flutter en masse, their blue so clear, so piercing as to be almost unearthly—or is it the association with Tibetan highlands that lends that aura of mystery? In any case, to see them is to want them. Be prepared for disappointment.

If I tell you that blue poppies, generally rated as hardy in zones 6 to 9, grow for us under the lilacs, you'll think I'm bragging. By process of elimination, we put them in a congenial spot at the start. Since then, my partner's careful ministrations—a bucket of water every three days during a summer drought and an annual feeding—have kept them content. Our initial meconopsis came from the Butchart Gardens in Victoria, British Columbia, by way of a gardening friend who bought a packet of seeds, raised two whole plants and gave us one. Since then, we've collected fresh seeds from the first clump and scattered them on the ground around it. Now there are four. The soil is dark and loamy, well drained and a little heavier than in the rest of the garden; each spring, it is top-dressed with compost. The site is cool and bright, shaded by shrubbery from about 11 a.m. on— no midday or afternoon sun—but not dark and close. The blue poppies never go thirsty.

Cool and moist may be the operative words. In the early 1900s, English botanical explorer and gardener Reginald Farrer admitted to trouble even in his balmy clime: "[Meconopsis] inhabit the mist zone of the [Himalayan] ranges and therefore enjoy conditions extraordinarily difficult to reproduce in England." And that much more difficult to duplicate in Ontario. To tell the truth—and maybe spare some heartache—if I gardened farther south, I wouldn't even try them; intense summer heat appears to be their nemesis.

Nothing ventured, nothing gained. Gardeners with a cool, shaded site— not dank or overhung with greedy trees, but fresh and breezy—might gamble a couple of dollars on a packet of fresh seeds or a robust small plant. If the planting site is routinely buried under snow over winter, so much the better. Be Zen about it: Enter into the task with a spirit of detachment and no expectations of success. Secure seeds or a starter plant (occasionally *Meconopsis* show up on a nursery bench, squeezed improbably between *Lychnis* and *Nepeta*). Work up the soil's humus content with thoroughly decayed leaves, fine compost, and the like. Haul out the watering can around the first of July. And pay your respects to Flora. Says one expert: "Their successful cultivation depends on providing them with living conditions exactly similar to those found in their natural habitat." All things considered, the West Coast is a more congenial home for meconopsis than the rest of the land, although I hear tell of a central-Quebec garden where meconopsis grow in profusion. As with all marginal perennials, results will vary from place to place, depending on conditions as localized as minor variations in soil and exposure, a fence, shrub or wall in just the spot where it will trap and hold snow, the right mulching material and that extra inch of it. In time, you become the expert in your own garden.

FACING PAGE: *A challenge to gardeners everywhere but especially those in hot, humid areas, the Tibetan blue poppy might be worth a try where cool, moist and lightly shaded conditions prevail.*

The Art of Perennial Gardening

Classic Duet

ROSES AND CLEMATISES

"A garden without a Rose is
a contradiction in terms."

RICHARDSON WRIGHT

FACING PAGE: *Light and dark—the*
wine-red petals of 'Sunset' clematis
stand out boldly among pale pink
'New Dawn' roses.

ABOVE: *Roses red, violas blue—a*
vigorous climbing rose, 'Red Flame'
wreathes a corner of a cedar arbor,
inviting a sniff as you go by.

STOPPING MIDWAY THROUGH A TOUR OF our garden to rest on a bench under a vine-draped arbor, our old neighbor sighed, "*Ah, je langer, je lieber.*" The longer you linger, the more you like it. One of the most enjoyable things to do in a garden is nothing—just sit, look and listen. In the usual rounds of busyness, so much goes unheeded. But in moments of stillness and quiet, you begin to notice slight sounds and movements: a redstart hopping through the honeysuckle, bumblebees droning from bugloss to borage, a monarch perched on the butterfly bush sipping nectar and drying its wings in the morning sun. Slipping into reverie, you find yourself caught by the luminescence of daffodils, a waft of scent from lilies, the lacquered crimson of highbush cranberries, the sway and whisper of grasses.

A bowered seat is one of the most pleasant adjuncts to a garden—a place for taking it all in. Arbored gateways, fences, trelliswork: These, too, bestow a sense of shelter and containment; they define space and make a garden more livable. But such niceties aside, the real reason gardeners erect posts, cross beams and trellises is to give their vines something to climb on. After going to the considerable work of building an arbor, the first thing we think about is how to cover it up.

Compared with shrubs and perennials, there are precious few vines that will survive and thrive in a northern garden. Those that do may be so rampageous—Virginia creeper comes to mind—that they will swallow a modest-sized arbor in a summer, then aim their tentacles at anything within reach. Without constant attention, grapevines shoot wildly in all directions. Strong-growing bittersweet is beautiful only when its red-and-yellow seedpods split in late fall, while honeysuckle vines resist our best efforts to coax them up a trellis and then fall prey to aphids. North of zone 6, wisteria is practically hopeless. What we can grow, however— not only up trellises and over arbors but also through rosebushes, shrubs and small trees—is clematis, very best of vines. (You say clem-*a*-tis, I say *clem*-a-tis; only don't say clem-*eye*-tis, rhymes with bronchitis.)

QUEEN OF VINES

Anyone who walks along the tree-lined streets of older town or city neighborhoods has seen sheets of deep violet clematis draping the porch pillars of some houses. This is the old Jackman's clematis (*Clematis jackmanii*), prototype of the group and a vine that embodies all we want in a climbing plant: hardiness, strong

FACING PAGE: *A clematis will climb on practically anything; here, 'Pink Chiffon' scrambles over nothing more elaborate than some dead twiggy branches pushed into the ground.*

LEFT: *Starting over from ground level each spring, 'Pink Chiffon' clematis wends its way up strings and through a 'Trier' rosebush; many other combinations of climbing roses and clematis vines work equally well.*

but not strangling growth, good health, gorgeous flowers and sumptuous color. No wonder it has been popular for over 100 years.

I don't know why it took us so long to realize that clematis could be tucked into any number of nooks and corners around our garden. But once we understood that the vines will scramble through whatever is nearby and fling their flowers over pillar and post, rosebush and apple tree, there was no stopping us. Making up for lost time, we have planted three or

four new clematis vines—large-flowered sorts and simple species—each spring for the past three years. In their array of purple, pink, mauve, violet, crimson and white, the large-flowered varieties have the most obvious appeal. The dainty species in muted shades of lavender, rose and white look like fairy caps, their narrow petals jauntily twisted and curled back. Scores of clematis vie for a gardener's attention. When confusion sets in, I remind myself that any is worth trying, and then I choose a

random sampling. Deep violet and cool lavender cultivars match all color schemes; but I try to keep mauve, purple and magenta away from yellow, orange and scarlet flowers. If colors get mixed up, so be it— I'd rather have a clematis that clashes than none at all.

What I'd rather not have is a clematis that wilts. Clematis diseases are few, but the one that gets around is infuriating enough. Clematis wilt is a mysterious ailment that strikes suddenly. Healthy one day, a vine may wither so quickly, you'd think it had been sliced off at ground level. Sometimes only a shoot or two will wilt, sometimes the whole plant. To a gardener's great frustration, wilt often attacks when a clematis is loaded with buds. Some say that the fungus comes with the plant itself, taking hold where vines are propagated for sale. In support of that the-

ory, I have noticed that certain "brands" seem more likely to wilt than others. (It would be unfair to name names, as one supplier may clean up its act while another is hit with the fungus.) Although wilted shoots never recover, healthy new shoots often develop from below soil level—especially if the vine has been deeply planted, as described below. Do not hastily dig up a wilted clematis. Prune back afflicted shoots immediately, right to ground level or even below, and daub a little pruning paste on the wound. With luck, things will be different next year.

Experts agree that wilt most often affects the fancier varieties with the largest flowers. Many of these bloom on growth made the previous year, woody strands that may not survive a hard winter. In an effort to circumvent both wilt and winterkill, we have been concentrating lately on

the ones that are cut back in late fall or early spring like any perennial. Here is a sampling: Old *jackmanii* is well regarded for its vigorous growth and masses of violet flowers. 'Gypsy Queen,' which has lived for a dozen years at Larkwhistle with little attention, sports larger violet blooms enhanced by reddish stamens. Flowering in August and continuing into September, medium-sized 'Huldine' is pearly white with a faint flush of mauve showing through from the back of its petals; in our Quiet Garden, it clambers over clumps of gooseneck flowers and snakeroot, their white spikes a fine contrast for the starry clematis blooms. Rambling up a shady arbor, 'Pink Chiffon' hangs out light mauve flowers, scores one year, a handful the next. Like the others, reddish 'Ville de Lyon' and 'Crimson King' are best cut back hard every year.

Recently we have been impressed with the performance of clematises belonging to the viticella group. All have smaller flowers—but masses of them—and seem to possess the most amazing health and vigor. All are cut back almost to the ground in November or April. The first we grew (on the recommendation of an expert who praised it as practically wiltproof) was *Clematis viticella* 'Étoile Violette.' After one season, the vines were completely covered with flowers indeed like violet stars. Discovered in Poland in 1984, the deep violet 'Polish Spirit' is lauded as "almost impossible to kill"—that's what we like to hear—and every summer, it shoots from the ground to the eaves of our garden shed, creating a column of color against the gray stone. 'Mme Julia Correvon' displays dark reddish purple flowers, 'Royal Velour' blooms burgundy, and 'Abundance' is larger and leans more to watered wine. Having had such good success with these, we mean to try any viticella that comes along. Cut back every spring, all begin to flower in July and continue through August. Their dusky colors add richness and depth to plantings of perennials and roses.

Clematis vines are natural scramblers, adept at pulling themselves toward the sun, leaf over leaf, grasping the twigs of neighboring plants like rungs of a ladder. It's a trait we can put to decorative use. Several of our flowerbeds are presided over by small ornamental trees—crabapples, Montmorency cherries, a tree (or standard) form of peegee hydrangea. At the base of each is a clematis. Sometimes the young tree and new vine are planted at the same time. A few strings guide the clematis into the tree's lower branches; after that, it's on its own. May brings apple and cherry blossoms; in July, the same trees erupt in clematis bloom. You need to be careful, though, when teaming a clematis with a small tree. Our standard hydrangea grew at a

snail's pace its first season, while the attendant clematis took off wildly, obliterating the hydrangea's every twig under its own foliage and flowers—and prompting one of our visitors to comment in all seriousness that he had never seen a "clematis tree" and to ask where he could get such a thing. Needless to say, the small hydrangea was not helped by the clematis's overwhelming embrace.

Of all clematis colors, I find dark violet, an intense but neutral shade worn by many of them, most useful for blending with other flowers. Violet clematises are luscious with the fruit shades of daylilies, red bergamot, white Shasta daisies and salmon yarrow. The same clematis is equally effective hanging above pink bergamot, pink and white Asiatic lilies, purple coneflowers, lavender pincushion flowers, deep rose *Veron-*

ica 'Red Fox' and similar hues of midsummer. In one bed, violet 'Gypsy Queen' clematis climbs the stalks of monkshood and dangles its big stars among aconite flowers of exactly the same color. Elsewhere, it mingles with the fluffy pink panicles of queen of the prairie (*Filipendula rubra*). Next spring, I plan to tuck 'Étoile Violette' among clumps of lemon daylilies and

FACING PAGE: *A clematis vine may sport large, showy flowers (the deep violet jackmanii) or smaller, more subtle blooms (pink 'Duchess of Albany'). As long as they have something to climb on, the vines take their place beautifully with other midsummer perennials—coral bells, Shasta daisies, red bergamot, daylilies and hollyhocks.*

LEFT: *The simple blooms of Clematis x durandii pick up a deeper tone of the color of the milky bellflower, Campanula lactiflora.*

The Art of Perennial Gardening

center) mixed with two handfuls of bone meal, a slow-acting fertilizer that will be available when roots stretch down. Clematis needs sweet ground, so avoid peat moss, which will acidify the soil to the vine's detriment. To the pile of topsoil add two handfuls of bone meal, one of blood meal and one of horticultural lime. If the topsoil is naturally acidic, add an extra dollop of lime. Mix the fertilizers with the topsoil, stirring well. Clematises want a rich, crumbly loam: If the existing topsoil is heavy and dense or very light and sandy, amend it with a spadeful of fine compost, very old manure or thoroughly rotted leaves, or bring in some store-bought earth. Gritty sand will help cut clay. Fill the hole with the amended topsoil—steal some from other parts of the garden if you need more—and tamp gently.

There is no need to choose a big, expensive clematis in a large container in hopes of quick results. Smaller plants in 5- or 6-inch pots will acclimatize readily and prove the better buy in the long run. The young vine should have a foot (1 m) or so of healthy growth and three to six stems. Tip the clematis carefully out of its pot. Roots may be wound around and tied together like boot-laces. If so, untangle them gingerly so that you can spread them out naturally. In the prepared zone, trowel out a hole deep enough that the rootball will be well down and 3 or 4 inches (8 to 10 cm) of the vine's stems will also be underground when the hole is filled. Planting depth is important: In the event of wilt, buried stems (which may sprout roots of their own) will renew the life of the clematis with fresh shoots. Fill in around the roots with soil, poking with your fingers to eliminate air pockets. Top up the hole with earth, and press firmly with your palms. Sculpt a wide basin around the plant, and fill it several times with water.

Unfasten clematis stems from the

let the vine ramble through them at will; I can picture the yellow trumpets interspersed with dark stars—light and shadow.

PLANTING CLEMATIS

A clematis vine may well be in place for decades, so spending half an hour preparing a planting spot should not be considered an unreasonable investment of your time.

Choose a position in full sun or light shade. Consider what the vine will climb on—trellis, fence, shrub, rosebush or even a pillar in the midst of a perennial bed. If the potted vine seems dry, soak it in a bucket of water while you prepare the place. Dig a hole roughly as deep and wide as a bushel basket. Put topsoil to one side, and if you encounter subsoil on your way down, pile it separately for later addition to the compost or another use. Break up the soil in the bottom of the hole, and shovel in two spadefuls of well-rotted manure (horse, cattle or sheep, from farmyard or garden

clip or band that is holding them together, and fan them out. At this stage, it is recommended that you shorten spindly top growth, cutting just above the lowest pair of buds. It's a step we may or may not take, depending on mood. Even knowing that side branches will develop, it takes a steely-minded gardener to nip off those tender tips. Clematis roots like to be cool and shaded. Lightly rooted dwarf plants around the base of the vine will do the job, but slabs of flat stone are better; an organic mulch may be best of all. I am reluctant to suggest a mulch of compost unless you know that the heap has fired up hotly enough to destroy infectious organisms. I'd use sterile commercial manure, bark or cocoa bean hulls instead and scratch in two handfuls of bone meal or equivalent fertilizer every spring. A fall mulch of manure keeps the vines vigorous. Water deeply and faithfully once a week during dry spells, and your clematis should thrive like the proverbial oak.

The Art of Perennial Gardening

A SAMPLING OF ROSES

Besides climbing fences and trellises, a clematis might be encouraged to grow through any shrub or tree of open structure: serviceberry, magnolia, viburnum, purple smokebush, purple-leafed plum or lilac, to name a few. Roses, though, are classic partners for clematis, not only lifting the vines into the light but often flowering in tandem with them. Pink, light blue, wine or white clematis stands out against the foliage of *Rosa rubrifolia* (syn. *glauca*), a tall shrub grown mainly for its dusky plum leaves and fall hips. Any of the viticella clematises can be set beside old-fashioned roses—sometimes called antique or historical—so that the simple stars will float among the plump roses. Violet clematises harmonize with all rose colors. After many years, I am still partial to *Rosa gallica versicolor* 'Rosa Mundi,' with its fragrant semi-double blooms streaked and splashed with crimson, pink and white. If a long association with gardens is a mark of a plant's beloved status, consider that 'Rosa Mundi' has been around since 1580. A mere parvenu from 1809, 'Koenigin von Dänemark,' is a favorite too, for highly perfumed, pure pink flowers of the classic old-rose shape—round, full-petaled and quartered; it is classified as an alba. In the same group (but 50 years younger) is 'Mme Legras de St. Germain,' with blushing white roses all the more beautiful with burgundy clematis 'Abundance' weaving through them.

In the spinosissima rose class, you find 'Stanwell Perpetual,' developed in France in 1838. Its light pink roses are borne from June to September on canes as spiny as the Latin implies. This willowy shrub is better set in a triangle of three plants on 2-foot (60 cm) centers. 'Gypsy Queen' clematis will pick its way through 'Stanwell Perpetual' and show darkly among the pale roses. Antique roses are a vast and confusing lot. Colors are limited to red, white, magenta and all shades of pink from blush to deep rose. Most flower exuberantly for a few weeks in early summer; some proffer a small fall encore. For hardiness and disease resistance, look among cultivars listed under alba and spinosissima; the centifolia and gallica groups also hold a number of winter-hardy varieties.

There seems to be an impression that roses must be grown by themselves in a special bed—what one writer calls "the asylum approach," in which roses are "restricted to the rose ward, under strict sanitary precautions." For those requiring winter bundling, drastic spring pruning and frequent summer sprayings—hybrid teas, grandifloras and floribundas—an exclusive setting facilitates care. Antique roses, by contrast, adapt to life amid the democratic jumble of a mixed border; indeed, other flowers bring out the best in them. Besides clematis, there are a number of potential companions for old-fashioned roses. Members of the onion family—garlic and chives—are traditional and may discourage some bugs. The ornamental onion *Allium christophii* hovers like an alien spacecraft among roses, as do the taller lilac-purple alliums 'Globemaster' and 'Beau Regard.' Lady's mantle might go in front for its dew-span-gled, pleated foliage and froth of chartreuse. Coral bells, too, grow lovely leaves and sprays of pink or red at the edge. The deep purples and blues of perennial salvias (varieties of *Salvia* x *superba*) set off pink and crimson roses, as do the blue and white blossoms of peach-leaved bellflowers (*Campanula persicifolia*). Foxgloves ascend behind rosebushes, while clusters of small lavender-blue bells belonging to tall *Campanula lactiflora* ring in the air above. Lavender exudes its warm scent in front of roses, and the silver of artemisia and lamb's ears is always welcome; billowing hardy geraniums contribute all-season foliage and flowers. Where roses grow in a mixed border, see that they are not smothered by perennials pressing in closely on all sides. Give a young rose a clear 3 feet (1 m) all around at the start, and allow other plants to encroach gradually as the rose fills out. Many perennials have the loose waywardness of meadow flowers (which, indeed, many of them are); they tend to fidget and flop. A few rosebushes help stabilize and anchor a flowerbed.

Beyond the antiques are other care-free shrubby roses to work in among perennials. We have had only pleasure from 'Sea Foam'; pushing 20 years old, our bushes remain robust and floriferous still. Clusters of blush-pink double flowers—round, saucer-shaped and beautiful in bud—adorn arching canes armed with reddish thorns; foliage is shiny and dark green, and new leaves are outlined in crimson. One of our young friends dubbed this the "raspberry rose" for its fruity fragrance. From July until well past Thanksgiving, 'Sea Foam' is never without flowers. Growing in the second row of sunny beds, our bushes are edged with pinks, lavender or 'Silver Mound' artemisia. As a precautionary measure in November, we incline the pliant branches, often still blooming, as close to the ground as possible and hold them down with

rocks; at that level, they are more likely to be blanketed with snow. Antique roses receive the same treatment. Even if some canes are killed, new shoots rebound vigorously and bloom the same year.

Easiest of all roses to grow—healthy, hardy as iron and unappetizing to most insects—are rugosa roses, hybrids (naturally enough) of *Rosa rugosa*. Their thick-textured, slightly crinkled leaves ("rugose" to a botanist) are medium green and glossy behind pink, white or reddish purple roses, either single or double. Pure pink and very tall, 'Jens Munk' is my favorite. At 4 feet (1.2 m), 'Scabrosa' is more contained and blooms on and off all summer; its simple flowers—five mauve-pink petals around a tuft of pale yellow stamens—give way to plump orange rosehips. For an easy duet of mauve and violet, position clematis 'Étoile Violette' or 'Venosa Violacea' to crawl over this rose. Single white rugosa roses exhibit a rare simplicity and make a lovely ladder for a pink or wine clematis.

Nothing infuses a garden with an air of romance like climbing roses fanning over fences and trellises or wrapping an arbor in bloom. In colder areas like ours, climbers take some extra effort, but it is work we willingly do. I cannot imagine a better climbing rose than 'New Dawn.' Our old bushes retain the vigor and beauty of their youth and delight us every summer with showers of pale pink apple-scented roses. The leaves are glossy, dark and invariably healthy, and (knock on wood) we have never encountered so much as a worm or an aphid on them. The perfect climber, except for one small detail. Every October, the great thorny thing must be untied and disentangled from its supporting structure and carefully bent—coaxed, eased, maneuvered—to the ground. It's a job that wants strong leather gloves and a snagproof jacket—and no one who is easily offended within earshot. Once the canes are as close to the ground as they'll go without snapping—our bushes have been up and down so often, I believe they have developed something like hinges—we weight them down with flat rocks or cement blocks. The next step involves carting four or five wheelbarrow loads of earth from the vegetable garden and completely covering the rose. Then it's *adiós* until spring, when the whole procedure is done in reverse order—plus pruning to shape and shorten live wood and cut out the dead. Protected branches emerge green and lively, while any tips that have poked through the soil cover are invariably dark and dead.

The same story applies to all our climbing roses—no problem except for the annual burial and resurrection. 'Illusion' and 'Red Flame' are crimson climbers of classic swirled shape; each rose—and there is never an explosion—is like a gift. I read good things about the Canadian-bred climber 'Henry Kelsey.' Said to be "the best red…for cold areas," it does not need the up-and-down treatment. Creamy white climbing rose 'Ilse Krohn Superior' might entwine with wine-red clematis. For a glorious show, plant a violet clematis—choose one that gets cut down each year—a little way away from the base

of 'New Dawn' rose. You want the clematis out in the open, not lost under the rose or stuck between it and a fence. Train the fast-growing vine up a few thin canes, twiggy branches or string until it grabs hold of the rose's lower stems, then let it run.

For years, a number of tough old farm flowers survived unattended in the field that has become our garden. Weaving through the tangle of daffodils and daylilies, sinewy rose canes ventured a halfhearted flower show. Intrigued by the bunches of small pink blooms, we replanted a chunk of the bush beside a newly built trellis. In the rich soil, the rejuvenated rose took off. Flexible and unbranched, its new canes were unlike any we had seen. The first summer, nary a flower; the next, a flamboyant display of pink and another set of long whiplike shoots. Dipping into our old gardening books, we identified the rose as a rambler, most likely 'Dorothy Perkins.' In habit, a rambling rose is like a raspberry: Canes that grow one year bloom the next and then gradually die out. To prevent a wild snarl, the canes that have flowered are cut away at ground level in the fall, leaving the current crop for next summer's color. For 20 years now, Dorothy has danced to the same rhythm up and down the same trellis. In late fall, after the old canes are cut, we lay the new batch down on the ground, looping them around on themselves. A few inches of snow seem to be all the protection this hardy rose needs—and, for summer company, a purple clematis.

SPECIES CLEMATIS

All through the northern temperate regions, from North America to the Far East, wild clematises grow in woodland clearings, through shrubs on mountain slopes and along hedgerows and roadsides, where they festoon other vegetation with their twisting vines and flurry of flowers.

FACING PAGE: *In June, the metallic lilac-gray stars of ornamental onion, Allium christophii, and the deep violet spikes of salvia 'East Friesland' contrast in both color and form with fluffy, pale yellow 'Agnes' roses; a rugosa hybrid, the rose is hardy well into the north.*

The Art of Perennial Gardening

Picturesque local names attest to the affection that folks feel for them. In France, one species is called *berceau de la vierge*, which has an English counterpart in virgin's bower. The Italian *barbagrigia* is "graybeard," in reference to the fluffy gray seedheads produced by many species, while the English call it old man's beard, grandfather's whiskers, father time, hedgefeathers and traveler's joy. Pleasant company for all who take to country lanes and footpaths.

Room might be made in gardens of the curious for some of the clematis species. First to flower at Larkwhistle is the alpine virgin's bower (*Clematis alpina*) and several of its cultivars. In June, the thin vines hang out dainty, four-petaled lavender blooms like little lanterns, modest flowers that might go unnoticed by those drawn only to razzle-dazzle. We let the unpruned vine trail where it likes—over a rugosa rose, up the stems of coneflowers, through a peony—in a narrow border in the Quiet Garden. 'Pamela Jackman' and 'Francis Rivis' are larger alpines and darker in tone. 'Pink Flamingo' sports extra petals in white washed with orchid-pink. Growing in our Rosy Border looped simply around some twiggy brush, it bridges the gap between spring bulbs and June's roses and irises. 'Willy' is pale pink, 'Ruby' is rose, and there is a white alpine as well. All have mops of silken seedheads after flowering.

A little later comes the Chinese species *Clematis macropetala*. The flowers, with slightly larger petals (as the Latin suggests), tip up to reveal their white centers. Named varieties are usually grown in preference to the original. The lavender 'Maidwell Hall' doubles its petals, as does the deeper blue 'Lagoon'; 'Markham's Pink' is rosy lavender, semidouble and nodding, and there is also a white cultivar. All grow from 8 to 12 feet (2.5 to 3.6 m) and will climb happily over whatever is at hand, be it trellis, fence, old stump or neighboring

plant. Sun or partial shade, it's all the same to these adaptable vines, and pruning is necessary only to shape and contain growth.

We have a splendid June clematis that seems to match the description of *Clematis recta*. Cut to the ground every fall, it reemerges with great vigor in spring, grasps the twine attached to a cedar arbor and hoists itself to a height of 6 feet (1.8 m). By early summer, the vine is smothered in thousands of small, pearly white, four- or five-petaled blooms with a

burst of creamy stamens. The effect is fluffy and light, a splendid contrast for early lilies, scarlet lychnis, roses and budding delphiniums nearby. Except for the annual cutting back, the vine is no work at all. Visitors seem to enjoy this clematis as much as we do.

The same arbor grows several varieties of *Clematis texensis*, vigorous climbers that display simple blossoms like small flaring tulips in midsummer. 'Duchess of Albany' is two shades of rose. In our overly rich soil,

FACING PAGE: *Historical roses such as striped 'Rosa Mundi' and pure pink 'Koenigin von Dänemark,' both brimming with fragrance, bloom for several weeks in early summer, making a romantic scene with foxgloves, coral bells, Siberian catmint and silvery artemisia.*

LEFT: *Like all rugosa roses, 'Hansa' is vigorous, healthy and exceedingly hardy; a spring pruning to shape the bush and remove damaged wood may be all the attention a rugosa needs.*

the vine runs to foliage at the expense of flowers—time to stop feeding the duchess. 'Sir Trevor Lawrence' is her crimson counterpart. Treated like any perennial, both are cut back hard in November. Given the distance covered in one season, I'd hate to think what they would engulf if allowed to spread unchecked. In the absence of a permanent trellis, these vines make do with a web of strings looped on nails hammered into the wooden arbor.

Coolly beautiful in the hot month of August is another herbaceous clematis, *C. heracleifolia davidiana,* and its cultivar 'Mrs. Robert Brydon.' At home in a perennial bed, the bushy plants reach only 3 feet (1 m) and top leafy stems with clusters of clear blue, sweetly scented flowers shaped like hyacinths. Cut to the ground in fall, they repeat the performance every summer and, like many clematises, grow increasingly showy with the passing seasons. One of our nicely established plants was eaten to shreds—stems, crown and some

roots—by an unidentified rodent. Because this clematis can be hard to find, we left the remains in place, hardly hoping for a comeback. Surprisingly, the few bits of gnawed root made a gradual recovery.

I doubt that anything short of a bulldozer could destroy the stalwart clematis that brings each Larkwhistle season to a close with a grand flowery finale. Years ago, we planted a root of *Clematis paniculata*, a climber with the lyrical name of sweet autumn clematis. "Piña colada" was how one of our helpers remembered the Latin; what he would make of the new surname, *maximowicziana*, I'm not sure. To add to the confusion, a recent catalog lists it as *C. terniflora*.

Let the botanists puzzle. The vine itself suffers no identity crisis; it knows exactly what it is about. In spring, strong shoots emerge from underground and head right for the trellised fence behind. Over the next two months, they weave their way to the top and then begin to clamber over the adjoining arbor, fanning out in both directions—a wall and ceiling of green spanning 15 feet (4.5 m). In late August, buds form, and by mid-September, sheets of small white flowers—some cross-shaped, others five-petaled stars—cascade over arbor and fence, filling the air with a delicate perfume reminiscent of almonds. Our autumn clematis shares a long arbor with a Virginia creeper and trails its white-clad arms over the fall-red foliage of its neighbor with fine effect. The two vines interlace over the entrance to the Quiet Garden, where white Japanese anemones and the red hips of a rugosa rose echo the colors at a lower level.

My mind's eye sees a fantasy fall scene. A long, high fence is draped with the green-and-white of sweet autumn clematis. In a narrow border below are clumps of Japanese anemones, both white and orchid-pink, interspersed with purple fall asters and pale yellow gladiolus. I might be tempted to slip in some orange torch lilies. For, as Louise Beebe Wilder notes, "However we may feel about strong color during the . . . summer, there are few who do not welcome it in the autumn garden. It is as if we wished to fill our souls with warmth and gaiety against the time when winter with its cold white silence shall lie upon the land." Swarming along the edge of my imaginary border are masses of colchicums, rosy mauve goblets like grandiose crocuses that spring up unexpectedly without foliage—they are sometimes called naked ladies—after fall rains. Nothing all summer and then this magnificent show, con-

tradicting rumors that the season for flowers is over.

Which, of course, it soon shall be. If not today, then next week or the next, a north wind will usher in a sky full of gray clouds and flurries. Not yet. A certain wistfulness hangs over the garden now, a sweet, sad melancholy that belongs to fall and endings—to transitions. The maple trees, yesterday fiery bouquets of scarlet, yellow and coral, have lost their leaves to a dousing overnight rain. But now, the sun is warm again. Gratefully we turn to whatever sparks of color remain in the garden. At a border's edge, a few brilliant orange California poppies, tricked by the "blue and gold mistake" of Indian summer, expand silken petals above a wave of sweet alyssum. Tireless Johnny-jump-ups, always the last to leave the party, convene a small chorus in a sheltered corner, and in the big terra-cotta pots on either side of the bowered seat, violas wave their blue banners—not a surrender but a dare. Looking like June flowers come late, Japanese anemones split their pearly buds; on into October, the four-petaled white flowers centered with a brush of yellow stamens—essence of simple beauty—sway in the wind. The last roses swirl open, summer distilled in their scent.

The silver blade has not touched sweet autumn clematis, which flowers blithely on despite many frosty nights. We admire the white mantle slung over the arbor, flower flakes piled up on themselves like a bank of—never mind. Time enough for that in January. Next spring, we will cut the great twisted vine to the ground and pull down the crackling dead stems in a shower of dry leaves. Its roots will be alive, though. Before you know it, the cycle will begin again.

SOURCES

AIMERS
81 Temperance Street
Aurora, Ontario
L4G 2R1
(905) 841-6226
Seeds and bulbs for domestic and wildflowers, including rare and unique seeds. Catalog $4.

BRICKMAN'S BOTANICAL GARDENS
RR 1
Sebringville, Ontario
N0K 1X0
(519) 393-6223
Over 3,000 species of perennials, specializing in rare hostas, cosmos, daylilies, peonies and irises. Catalog $2, refundable.

THE BUTCHART GARDENS, LTD.
Box 4010
Victoria, British Columbia
V8X 3X4
(250) 652-4422
Old-fashioned perennials. Catalog $1, refundable.

CRUICKSHANK'S INC.
780 Birchmount Road, Unit 16
Scarborough, Ontario
M1K 5H4
(416) 750-9249
Specialists in flowering bulbs and other flowering perennials. Four-season catalog subscription $3.

DOMINION SEED HOUSE
Box 2500
Georgetown, Ontario
L7G 5L6
(905) 873-3037
Flower and vegetable seeds, bulbs, plants and rooted cuttings of flowering plants. Catalog free.

GARDENIMPORT INC.
Box 760
Thornhill, Ontario
L3T 4A5
(905) 731-1950
Perennial plants, bulbs and flowers. Stock unusual perennials. Catalog $5 for two years, refundable.

GARDENS NORTH
5984 Third Line Road N., R.R. 3

North Gower, Ontario
K0A 2T0
(613) 489-0065
Seeds for hardy perennials, rare and common. Catalog $4.

HALIFAX SEED CO. INC.
Box 8026
5860 Kane Street
Halifax, Nova Scotia
B3K 5L8
(902) 454-7456
Flower, herb and vegetable seeds. Catalog free in Canada.

MCCONNELL NURSERIES
Box 248
Strathroy, Ontario
N7G 3J2
1-800-363-0901
Perennial flowers and bulbs as well as other plants. Catalog free.

MCFAYDEN SEED CO. LTD.
30-9th Street, Suite 200
Brandon, Manitoba
R7A 6N4
1-800-205-7111
Seeds and hardy perennial flower plants for short-season gardens. Catalog free.

PARK SEED COMPANY
Cokesbury Road
Greenwood, South Carolina 29647-0001
1-800-845-3369
Flower, vegetable and herb seeds, including perennials. Catalog free.

PEEK'S PERENNIALS
Box 6443
Edson, Alberta
T7E 1T8
(403) 723-5701
Hardy perennials, including many unusual varieties. Catalog $2 for two years, refundable.

RAINFOREST GARDENS
13139-224th Street
Maple Ridge, British Columbia
V4R 2P6
(604) 467-4218
A good selection of organically grown herbaceous perennials, especially shade varieties. Catalog $4 for two-year subscription.

SELECT SEEDS—ANTIQUE FLOWERS
180 Stickney Hill Road
Union, Connecticut 06076
(860) 684-9310
Hardy perennial heirloom flower seeds; vintage flowers. Catalog $2 U.S. or Canadian money order.

SHERRY'S PERENNIALS
Box 39-W
Cedar Springs, Ontario
N0P 1E0
(519) 676-4541
Many shade-tolerant and long-blooming perennial plants. Catalog $4 for two years, refundable.

SOUTH COVE NURSERY, LTD.
Box 615
Yarmouth, Nova Scotia
B5A 4B6
(902) 742-3406
Perennials, ground covers and herbs. Catalog $2.

STIRLING PERENNIALS
RR 1, Dept. CG
Morpeth, Ontario
N0P 1X0
(519) 674-0571
Hardy perennial plants. Catalog free.

STOKES SEEDS LTD.
39 James Street, Box 10
St. Catharines, Ontario
L2R 6R6
(905) 688-4300
Seeds for flowers, herbs and vegetables. Catalog free.

THOMPSON & MORGAN, INC.
Dept. PR98
Box 1308
Jackson, New Jersey 08527
1-800-274-7333
An excellent selection of seeds of common and unusual perennials. Parent company is British. Catalog free.

FURTHER READING

Davies, Dilys. *Alliums: The Ornamental Onions*. Timber Press, Portland, Oregon, 1992.

Lima, Patrick. *The Harrowsmith Perennial Garden: Flowers for Three Seasons*. Camden House, Camden East, Ontario, 1987.

Osborne, Robert. *Roses for Canadian Gardens*. Key Porter, Toronto, 1991.

Perényi, Eleanor. *Green Thoughts: A Writer in the Garden*. Vintage, New York, 1981.

Phillips, Roger and Martyn Rix. *The Random House Book of Perennials*. Random House, New York, 1991.

Pizzetti, Ippolito and Henry Cocker. *English Flowers: A Guide for Your Garden*. Abrams, New York, 1975.

Robinson, Mary A. *Primulas: The Complete Guide*. Crowood Press, Swindon, Wiltshire, England, 1990.

Thomas, Graham Stuart. *Perennial Garden Plants; or The Modern Florilegium*. Dent, London, 1976.

Wilder, Louise Beebe. *My Garden*. Doubleday, Page & Company, New York, 1916.

Wilder, Louise Beebe. *Colour in My Garden*. Doubleday, Page & Company, New York, 1918.

Wilder, Louise Beebe. *Adventures with Hardy Bulbs*. Macmillan, New York, 1936.

INDEX